MENTALLY STRONG

7 Steps *to* Becoming *the* Best Version *of* Yourself

Freddy Sandoval

Mentally Strong
© 2020 by Freddy C. Sandoval

ISBN (Print): 978-1-09833-361-4
ISBN (eBook): 978-1-09833-362-1

To Kaleb and Micah:
So you know that
if you believe and turn your
thoughts into action,
you can achieve anything!

Endorsements

"I have known Freddy since we were both kids playing baseball in Tijuana, and I know he has always been a person that analyzes and takes the mental part of the game of baseball and puts it into play. Having worked with him during my professional career I know and understand how important it is to work on your mentality, not just in the game of baseball but in life. Freddy does an incredible job on this book taking his work and vision, and providing everyone with a very simple way to exercise the mind. The principles and steps of Mentally Strong will strengthen anyone's mind and will lead anyone who reads it to individual success in sports and in life. This book is a difference-maker. Freddy congratulations, I am so proud of you and I know this book will help a lot of people when they read it. It will not only transform people's mentalities, but also their lives."

–**Adrian Gonzalez**, *15-year MLB career, 3-year LMP career*

"We all need first responders; a person with specialized training who is amongst the first to arrive and provide assistance at the scene of an emergency. At the lowest point of my life and professional career, that person became Freddy Sandoval. He arrived at my scene and explained how to apply the principles of this book. The principles that would change the outcome of my life. I experienced success both on and off the field overcoming my fears, anxiety, and discovering my self-worth. The principles which are now written in this book helped me overcome a third possible career-ending surgery and as a result leading me to have one of the best years as a pitcher in the Major Leagues. If you find yourself in need of a responder, I encourage you to read Mentally Strong. Its life changing principles will enable you to live a life with meaning and fulfillment."

–**Jaime Garcia**, *Author and 10-year MLB career*

"I've been blessed to call Freddy my Mental Coach, but above all he is an incredible human being with an intense desire to impact as many people's lives as possible. From the first day I met him, this book was a burning goal within his heart. As I read the book, I was so proud, because I knew it was the culmination of so many years of his personal journey, education, and passion to help others. As someone who has completed many steps of Freddy's training on a personal level, I loved the accessibility and simplicity of the steps laid out in this book. Thank you, Freddy, for this amazing labor of love."

—**Amy Thomas**, *Client and Hydrocephalus patient/advocate*

"Being in Professional baseball for over 30 years, I have experienced the mental challenges to be able to perform at a high level on a daily basis. I believe that building the mind is crucial to success. In Mentally Strong, Freddy provides mental training tools that are not only helpful to athletes, but for anyone who wants to improve in every area of life."

—**Bobby Magallanes**, *Bench Coach for the Atlanta Braves*

"After reading Mentally Strong, I am now more convinced that the mental side of life and sports is fundamental to success. This book is a well-defined manual that gives you the step by step instruction and tools to find perfect balance between the mind and the body. Freddy has gotten to the highest level as an athlete and as a mental coach and this book is a unique piece. If you are a person looking to turn your goals into reality and to turn your life around, this is the perfect book for you. I highly recommend Mentally Strong to anyone, in any stage of life to help you reach your goals, transform your mindset and prolong your well-being. "

—**Jorge Campillo**, *5 year MLB career*

Contents

Introduction

Ever since I can remember, I knew I wanted to become a professional baseball player. Growing up in Mexico, I wanted to play at the Major-League level in the United States, an accomplishment that very few Mexican players had achieved. To achieve this unique and crazy goal, I knew that I needed to have dedication, commitment, drive, and passion. And I knew I was going to sacrifice a lot of other things, such as family time and relationships with friends. However, for some time, my life and actions did not match up with my goals, and early in my career, my dream was derailed. It took a friend and an honest conversation for me to get back on track and finally start doing what I needed to do without excuses.

I owe a lot to this person because with a single conversation, he opened my eyes, and my life completely changed for the better. One conversation led me to start making better decisions and it was because I took action that I can now live the life I always wanted.

I've known Adrian Gonzalez since we were little kids. We met when we were only 4-5 years old, playing baseball in the fields of Liga Municipal de Tijuana. Although we were never teammates, we got to play together on some all-star teams through the years. Since then, we have been good friends, but I never realized *how* good of a friend he really was until one night in January of 2007.

I was drafted out of the University of San Diego by the Anaheim Angels in the 8th round of the 2004 First Year Major League Baseball draft. I was the 233rd pick overall, however, my professional career didn't start that year. I was drafted in 2004 but didn't play a single inning that year.

In 2004, the sport of baseball had restrictions as to how many visas each team could have for international players, and I didn't have a working visa that year. That same season, the Venados of Mazatlán selected me first overall in the Mexican Pacific League draft, but I ended up not joining the team the first year. Even though I had achieved the first step towards my goal of professional baseball, I had not yet played at all that first season.

Baseball has a unique system in which players who get drafted or who sign free-agent contracts go through the minor leagues to start their careers. It is in the minor leagues that players develop and hone their skills with the dream of making it to the big leagues. The system consists of different levels, where based on your talent and ability, you play with the hopes of playing at a high level while staying healthy. Most players start at the rookie-level, which can either be in the Dominican Republic, Arizona, or Florida, where the minor-league complexes are. There is no timeline as to how long you will play in each level because the organization's management is the one making decisions on your career. Based on your performance, they can either move you up to a different level, drop you down, or ultimately release you. The rookie level consists of two levels: rookie and advanced rookie. Next, is class single A, which also consists of two levels: class A and class A advanced. Then, if you are still healthy and performing well according to management's standards, you can be promoted to double-A. Lastly, triple-A is the last level before reaching the big leagues. As I mentioned before, there is no rule of thumb as to how you advance through the system. Many players have skipped levels and reached higher grounds sooner than expected while other players' careers have ended sooner than anticipated.

In 2005, I finally experienced my first season as a professional baseball player. I played in class single-A in Cedar Rapids, Iowa, where I had a good first season. Like life itself, it was full of ups and downs, but overall, I had a great season and I learned a lot. After the season, I headed down to Mazatlán, Mexico for the first time to continue developing as a player. In 2005, I had the opportunity to get my first Mexican Pacific League hit and also had the opportunity to be a part of a championship team.

In 2006, back in the United States, I was promoted to the single-A advanced team in Rancho Cucamonga, California. There, I had an okay season filled injuries and more ups and downs. Ultimately, though, it was an okay year. As I had done the previous year, after the season in the United States, I headed to Mazatlán to play Winter ball.

I say I headed to Mazatlán to play, but I rarely played. I was a rookie and I was sharing the field with players I admired and grew up watching. It was a great time for me to continue learning and developing as a player. In addition to playing a little, this is where I reconnected with my long-time friend Adrian Gonzalez.

The conversation that changed my life.

Adrian was already established in the Majors (U.S.) and came down to Mazatlán to continue crafting his skills and continue developing as a player in the Winter. It was the first season where I played more regularly in Mazatlán, but regardless of the stats and the accomplishments, my most important learning came after we beat Culiacan at home in Mazatlán during the semi-finals. After the game, the whole team went out to celebrate at one of the local bars. We were waiting to hear who we would play in the Mexican Pacific League Championship.

As we were celebrating, I was sitting on a table with a lot of my childhood idols who were now my teammates. Amongst them was Adrian Gonzalez. Baseball players talk baseball so we were making assumptions as to who we would play in the championship and whatnot. The conversation led, as usual, to talking about the game we had just played. Even though I hadn't played, our team had beat Culiacan in a dramatic fashion so there was a lot of adrenaline running through our blood and a lot of situations to talk about.

Before I continue with this story, let me say that Adrian is one of the most knowledgeable baseball guys I have ever known in my life and that he loves to talk baseball. While he was talking about the game, there was a moment when he looked to me in regards to a situation that had happened during the game, and I was clueless. Even though I had been there, I had no idea what he was talking about. Adrian continued talking more about the game and it was almost as if I had not been there at all. As I mentioned before, I didn't play in that game, but I also didn't remember a thing about it. Despite the fact that I was physically there, I wasn't there mentally. It was at that point that Adrian must have noticed something in me and before I knew it, he and I were having a separate conversation.

In that moment, Adrian talked to me as a baseball player and a teammate, but most importantly, he talked to me as a friend. Adrian asked questions no one had ever asked me before. The initial things he asked were about me, not about baseball or about how my baseball career was going. Instead, they were questions about how I was doing in my personal life and eventually, as we talked into the early morning hours, the conversation led back to how I was approaching my baseball career.

Adrian asked me, do you work out? "Mmm, yeah."

He followed up with, "How often?"

"Maybe two to three times a week," I responded with shame and guilt because of two reasons: 1) I knew how dedicated Adrian is and 2) because internally, I was disappointed in myself.

His response shocked me and changed the way I would live my entire life from that point forward.

"What happened to you?" It wasn't really a question. He cared enough to challenge me, and honestly, it couldn't have come from a more impactful person. He continued, "What happened to you? You used to be way better than me growing up, and now you are partying and going out all the time, and not paying attention to your life and your career. I already made it to the big leagues, and you are in high A. Do you really want to make it to the big leagues?"

I want to clarify that Adrian wasn't being arrogant or egocentric. Those of us that have the pleasure of knowing him know that he is the complete opposite. He is humble and loves to help people. On this particular occasion, that's exactly what he was doing - he was helping me. The conversation brought me back to earth and as a friend, Adrian reminded me that I was not doing what I needed to do to achieve my goals and live the life I wanted to live. Minutes into the conversation, I started crying. Tears started coming down my face because I knew in my heart that what Adrian was telling me was the truth. As the old saying goes, "Sometimes the truth hurts."

I remember clearly that as I was crying, I pushed my drink away. Adrian noticed and said, "Right now is about celebration. It's okay to celebrate tonight, but if you truly want to achieve your goal and make it to the big leagues, you might want to consider changing your ways."

This was the first time that someone had spoken to me like that - with heart, passion, and honesty. It hit home. Adrian talked to me about resilience, hard work, and commitment. Most importantly, he spoke about my character and changing my mentality. Over the next few days, our discussion continued, and Adrian pointed me in the right direction with workouts, meal plans, schedules, and routines. The rest is history.

That year, 2007, Venados of Mazatlán ended up losing game seven of the championship. It was a 1-0 game against Hermosillo. A few months later, back in the United States, I was once again promoted, this time to the double-A team. I headed to North Littlerock, Arkansas as a new man, with a renewed purpose, and with a stronger mentality. That year, I had great numbers, earning a place in the MLB Futures Game as well as receiving other personal awards. As I continued my transformation into a better life with a new mentality, in 2008 I was promoted to Triple-A in Salt Lake City, where I played and produced career-high numbers. I broke and tied some records and even earned the Anaheim Angels top honor, becoming Minor League Player of the Year. Then, on September 8th of the same year, 2008, my lifetime goal of reaching the big leagues became a reality.

To this day, I don't know what would have become of me if not for that incredible conversation with Adrian Gonzalez. I am thankful to him in a lot of ways, not just because he saw me at a low point in my life and had the right words to say to me, but because he planted the first seed in my mind about transformation. Most of my life, I was living and learning, making mistakes, failing, and being disappointed. Now, I approach life differently and each day I continue to learn, grow and become better at whatever it is that I am doing. I know each day comes with its own set of difficulties and challenges, but I am now more equipped to face those challenges with a strong mentality thanks to Adrian.

"A fifty percent effort,
will give you a fifty percent result."
Adrian Gonzalez

The Intent

Just as Adrian changed my way of thinking with a single conversation, I hope you read this book as if you are sitting down to talk with a friend. I want to provide you with the tools to change your way of thinking so you can live the life you want. With understanding and practical application, the tools and techniques I am going to introduce to you in this book will start a transformational change that will strengthen your mindset. A stronger mindset will lead you to live life with less tension and stress and maximize your potential.

The Approach

Read this book at your own pace understanding that each chapter is going to bring its own set of ideas, challenges, and ways of thinking. Take the time to grasp, process, and understand the information provided on each topic. Remember, this book is for you and the unique way that you apply the topics will directly influence your transformation.

The Program

After reading the book continue your journey with the 10-week Mentally Stronger Plan in the appendix. The proactive program will challenge you every week on one topic and one mentality. You are to work on each topic for one week to gain awareness, self-control, and, little by little develop a new habit. At the end of the 10 weeks, you will be well on your way to becoming the best version of yourself.

A Note from the Author

If you have ever been frustrated with the way you are living because it is not matching up with what you want to achieve in life, you are not alone.

I grew up believing in a quote that you have probably heard before, "Life is about the choices we make." As many others do, I lived my life focusing on the choices that were presented to me by other people or by chance. Instead of being proactive in my thinking and pushing myself to create a better future for myself, I simply let the choices that happened guide my life's path. Without realizing, I had lost control of myself and ignored my goals and my happiness. I didn't know any better. I made mistakes, went through failure, and was often disappointed in myself. But I wanted to believe there was more, and that I could achieve more and make the most of my opportunities. As I matured, I began understanding how the mind and body work and decided to live a better, happier life.

You see, there is a difference between a choice and a decision. Choices are just choices, options, and possibilities. A decision, however, is a conclusion or resolution after consideration of your choices. The problem is we often decide on a choice that doesn't line up with what we want and therefore, we feel unhappy with ourselves.

When you go to a restaurant, you are presented with different choices on the menu. Something as simple as a menu can be overwhelming and cause stress. However, at some point, you make up your mind and make a decision about what you want to eat or drink. That's the difference between choices and decisions. In a way, life works the same way. Life can be overwhelming and stressful as we look at the choices we have- but the real question is, what decisions are you going to make? Your transformation takes place in the decisions you make, so enjoy them and make the most of every choice you have.

In this book, my hope is that you will learn about things you didn't know before (which is awareness). You will learn, grow, and become better (be in control) and ultimately, you will live better (make better decisions). During this transformation, understand that ultimately, you have choices, and the decisions you make will dictate the path you take.

In a way, life is not about the choices we have—it is about the decisions we make, so always remember...

"You are only one decision away
from a complete different life."
Unknown.

MENTALLY STRONG

Principles

"Principles are what allow to live a life
consistent with those values. Principles
connect your values to your actions."
Ray Dalio

Before I introduce you to the main principles you are going to learn
about, I want to introduce you to the term "cognitive flexibility."
Cognitive flexibility, also referred to as "shifting," refers to our ability
to switch between different mental sets, tasks, or strategies. Shifting
is the ability to adjust one's thinking from old situations to new situations. As you are about to embark on this transformational journey,
I encourage you to approach this book with a clear, open mind.
Having cognitive flexibility stretches our mind to new ideas and new
possibilities. You may have already heard some of this information
before, but if you come to it with a clear mind, you will be able to
understand information from a different perspective. This book is not
meant to disrupt your spiritual beliefs; however, it is meant to provide
new ideas, beliefs, and mentalities that challenge your current belief
system so that you can become the best version of yourself.

In this section, I am going to introduce you to different principles,
theories, models, and mentalities. These three principles are a part

of my own belief system and are the foundation that I have found have greatly helped my mental training clients.

First Principle
"You don't know what you don't know."

The first principle is that we don't know what we don't know. If you think about it, it's a funny statement because it is obvious—but ultimately, it is true. This principle plays a huge role in how we approach our daily life. To put things in perspective, it is said that if you were to write down all the things that you know, and absolutely everything you believe in, you could write up hundreds of books because there are a lot of things that you know. However, if you were to write about all the things you don't know, you could write a library. The amount of information and things we don't know about is overwhelming. This book will dig deeper into things most of us don't pay much attention to, into things we take for granted, and the idea that you need to accept information you don't know to learn.

Behind this first principle, there is something I want you to consider - if you don't know something, how do you improve it? How do you make it better? Have you ever had an argument with someone and had no idea why they were upset with you? The funny thing is that 9 times out of 10, the other person knows what's bothering them and yet, they won't share the information with you. Subsequently, we can't fix it or make it better. This is an example of something that happens quite often, but what about all the things we don't know about? How about when we hurt or bother other people and we are completely unaware? This is where awareness comes in. Awareness is fundamental to recognize thoughts, actions and behaviors so that you can distinguish and change them. Gaining awareness is the goal behind the first principle.

Second Principle
"Learn, grow, and become better."

The second principle I want to mention is the principle of learning, growing, and becoming better. It is my belief that all people want to improve themselves in one way or another. Some lack motivation, desire, or drive, while others don't have guidance or have grown accustomed to living in a certain way. Many people have grown used to the bad habits they've developed or are just unwilling to change. But then, there are those people who are willing to do what needs to be done and change. This is the foundation of growth- to be willing to change and once you have that wish, you can learn, grow, and become better.

As you will learn in this book, the human mind is so power-ful. Just as easy as it is to learn something, you can also unlearn something. Learning new habits or unlearning undesired old habits applies to attitude, behavior, thinking patterns, and the physical body. I am not saying that this is an easy process. However, it is possible. If we truly want to change something about ourselves that we don't like, we have the power and the ability to change in many ways. When we learn something new, whether it is physical, a new game, or, in this case, new mentalities, we grow as human beings. Learning something new can also motivate you to incorporate the new information into your own life. As you learn, you grow, and when you grow, you become better than you were before.

Many of us have grown accustomed to expecting progress very quickly. We want the changes to happen immediately and not seeing progress can take us back to the place we started. This second principle focuses on constant growth. It doesn't matter how small or how large the growth is, it is about making sure that today you can be a little better than you were yesterday. That is progress and even a little progress is better than no progress. Little by little, that small progress will turn into bigger progress and, before you know it, you will learn. The new information is going to be instilled in your long-term memory and turn into new habits, leading you to be better than you were before.

All of us make mistakes but learning something means we know about it consciously and subconsciously, and it means we should not make the same mistake again. Albert Einstein said that "insanity is to repeatedly make the same mistake and expect a different result." Doesn't this sound like a lot of the mistakes we make? We are constantly expecting a different result without even looking at changing something in our life. So above all, this second principle to learn, grow, and become better, deals with being in control of your own mind.

Third Principle
"Learn to live."

The third principle has to do with what I made reference to in the conversation with Adrian. How many times have you heard someone say, "We live, and we learn?" It is a common phrase. Are we really going to go through life making mistakes so that we can learn something? What if we flip the words live and learn, and instead, we could constantly *learn* so that we can *live* better? This principle is what this book is all about. It's about gaining awareness and self-control so that we can proactively learn to have a different mindset. It is about changing the way we think so that we can live a better life moving forward.

Many of us are haunted with decisions we've made in the past, and we allow our past to dominate the way we act and think. Through awareness and self-control, you are going to learn to live a less stressful life. By paying attention to the things that matter and to the things you can control, you can have more clarity of your thinking. This is going to allow you to make the best possible decisions about your own life. The decisions we make on a daily basis create a blueprint for the life we build for ourselves and, as I mentioned before, we are always one decision away from a completely different life.

Ultimately, the information you learn plus the application of the concepts will change the way you look at the world. Being mentally strong is not just a mask you put on from time to time, it's a way of life… it's a lifestyle. This third principle will lead you to make better decisions so that you can get closer to your goals and achieve what you want for your life.

"There are three constants in life:
change, choice, and principles."
Stephen Covey

Theories

"We see the world
in terms of our theories."
Thomas Kuhn

I believe, the value and understanding behind some of the theories outlined in this book are essential to our growth and development as human beings. It is my suggestion that you refer to these theories as much as you need to so that you can fully comprehend and apply them to the concepts you are going to learn in the 7 steps of this book.

Leadership

The dictionary describes a leader as a person who leads or commands. It is my hope that as you read this book, you acquire the leadership skills to lead your own life. Then, once you start to take command of your life and move in the direction you want to go, you will influence and lead others to personal growth and transformation along the way.

Personality

As a professional coach and consultant, I believe it is important to have a basic understanding about personality, traits, and profiles. Personality is the characteristics or blend of characteristics that make a person unique. Specific personality traits focus on an individual's characteristics of thought, feelings, and behavior. A personality profile can help clarify a person's attributes, values, and life skills to maximize performance.

There are over two thousand different personality assessments in the United States alone. They are all a little different and each brings a different perspective to the table. Although I believe all personality traits, theories, and assessments are valuable in their own way, the one I recommend is the Myers Briggs Type Indicator (also known as "MBTI").

MBTI is considered the most accurate and most widely used personality assessment in the world. Upon completing the MBTI assessment, the participant can learn and analyze data based on up to 20 different areas of their personality. All of this is super helpful, especially for someone who has never taken a personality assessment before. In my work as a coach, I use it mostly as a communication and awareness tool. As a Myers-Briggs Type Indicator Certified Practitioner, I ask all my clients to take the fifteen-minute assessment to reveal their personality type. Based on the accuracy of the assessment, it allows me to effectively communicate with a client in a way that is specific to them and allows me to explain traits and behaviors that make up their particular type.

Personality assessments are not meant to discover who you are as a person, but more so to focus on specific traits that make up your personality. During this quest, you may discover new things about yourself or just reconfirm the individual qualities that form your distinctive character. Often, the most valuable takeaway from an assessment such as the MBTI is to have a better understanding of how you interact and communicate with other human beings. Simply validating who you are and how you feel in certain social and relationship scenarios can be a game-changer professionally and personally.

According to personality theories, you are who you are for the rest of your life. Personality does not change. What changes is your ability to make different decisions. For example, some of your personality traits might change over time, or mature as we often say, but the reason is because you actually made a different decision in regard to that trait. For example, I've always considered myself to be a very impatient person. Eventually I became a patient person, but it was a decision that was made during the process that allowed me to go from impatience to patience.

I encourage you to take a personality assessment prior to reading the steps in this book. Most assessments will take 5-15 minutes and will provide you with basic information about the traits that make up your personality.

*See appendix for more information on MBTI and for sources where you can take the assessment.

Communication

Communicating effectively is one of the most powerful tools you can have as an individual. In fact, research shows that you spend 80% of your time communicating. Although we spend most of our life communicating with those around us, we often communicate ineffectively, which ends up raising our stress levels. According to stress.org, 80% of people feel stressed because of ineffective or poor communication. In the third step to becoming the best version of yourself, we will go deeper into the art of communication. It is important to know that we will deal with ineffective communication later in this book in an effort to reduce stress and improve relationships.

Mind and Body Connection

There are lots of different theories about the mind and body connection and I encourage you to explore these theories and their relationship to each step on your own as you continue your learning. For the sake of this book and the theories I am presenting to you, I think it's important for you to have a basic understanding of a couple of concepts. The first is that the mind and the body are two different things. Simply stated, the mind is made up of thought and consciousness and second, the body refers to the physical aspects. In a perfect world, we want the mind and the body to work together, in perfect harmony and in synchrony so that the two entities can work as a single entity.

This book will introduce you to tools that can be used to join the mind and the body so you can live a better life. Actively working on your mind (thought and consciousness) will lead you to develop a stronger connection between the mind and the body. You will relieve tension and stress while also increasing your confidence. Doing the mental work I will outline for you in this book will condition your brain to discover and maximize your true potential. Other areas of improvement will be your self-talk, which is a reflection of your internal beliefs. I am going to teach you relaxation techniques so you can be more efficient and proficient in all areas of your day-to-day life, as well as in moments of pressure or performance. When you master the tools in this book, it will allow you to consistently enter a mind-flow state of mind, create proper muscle memory, instill new habits, develop a positive attitude, and ultimately change your behavior.

There is an incredible relationship between the mind and the body and through our thoughts, feelings, beliefs and attitudes, we can positively or negatively influence our biological functioning. What we do with our physical body can impact our mental state either positively or negatively. I know from personal experience how powerful it is when the mind and the body are working in sync, and I am excited to share this information with you—so you can start getting the most out of the work you put in.

Chevreul's Pendulum

There are different ways to exemplify the connection between the mind and the body. One of my favorites, because it's truly unbelievable, is the Chevreul Pendulum. Michel Chevreul was a well-known French natural scientist who investigated the "occult" (the realm of magical or mystical things), and who gave a plausible scientific explanation to the pendulum. A pendulum is an energy transferring device that can be simply made of a piece of thread with a small weight at one end. Pendulums have been used throughout history in many ways, from mechanics to artwork. Most commonly, people have seen a pendulum on a grandfather's clock. Today, I am going to explain how the pendulum is used to demonstrate the astonishing and remarkably strong effects of autosuggestion.

The Experiment

Sit down at a table and rest your elbow on the tabletop. Hold the pendulum or sewing thread between your thumb and forefinger, so that the pendulum weight (paper clip or ring) hangs straight down. Try holding the pendulum as still and immovable as possible. As the pendulum is hanging, imagine the pendulum starts to swing side--to--side. After 15 seconds to 3 minutes of intense imagining, the pendulum will start to swing left to right. If you order the pendulum to stop swinging and start imagining the pendulum swinging back and forth after seconds, the pendulum will start swinging back and forth.

Once again, start thinking how the pendulum comes to a complete stop and then start imagining again that the pendulum is now spinning in whatever direction you want it to spin. Once the pendulum starts to spin, imagine again that the pendulum comes to a stop and starts to swing in the opposite direction. Again, the pendulum will start to swing in the opposite direction.

I have had a lot of people ask me if this experiment is some type of black magic. However, investigations have discovered that it is not. The pendulum moves because of natural human reaction. Your body is full of energy, and at the order of your brain to make the pendulum swing in one direction, your brain sends signals to your body, signals that are not visible to the human eye. Responding to those orders, or energy signals, your body makes very small movements. The pendulum, being an energy-collecting device, collects these signals, or vibrations from your body and causes the pendulum to move.

The principle that was uncovered with Chevreul's investigation is that the human body reacts physically (and chemically) to imagined situations. In short, your body reacts to what you are thinking, and the pendulum is an amazing way to prove it.

Self-Fulfilling Prophecy

A self-fulfilling prophecy is defined as a prediction that causes itself to be true due to the behavior (including the act of predicting it) of the believer. Self-fulfilling means that it is brought about as a result of being foretold or talked about while prophecy refers to the prediction. This prophecy suggests that people's beliefs influence their actions.

In a way, the self-fulfilling prophecy suggests that whatever you believe about yourself is right. You could certainly be wrong in those beliefs. However, because you believe them to be true, the self-fulfilling prophecy says they are going to be true to you. If you think about it, most arguments start because people have different beliefs. You may believe one thing, but another person might have a different belief, therefore, leading to a discussion or argument. If we understand this concept correctly, both people are right in their own way because they both believe in what they believe in.

GIGO Principle

GIGO is a computer science acronym that stands for "garbage in, garbage out." The quality of the information that goes in, is the quality of the information that goes out. Simply put, bad input will result in bad output.

In this book, we will use and apply this computer science acronym and apply it to the mind and how we think. Many of us have, at one point or another, heard that the mind is like a computer. In many ways, the brain is like a computer. It processes, saves, and deletes information, data, numbers etc. Our bodies, as proven with the Chevreul's Pendulum are like a printer. Our bodies react to how we think.

If in a computer, I type 1+1=5 we know the result is wrong. However, if we print the result, we are going to print the wrong answer. It does not matter how many times we print that data, the information will always print out wrong because the information that was typed was wrong. In the same manner, if we intake negative or wrong information into our brain, our bodies are going to "print" the very same information we have in our mind. If we have negative information in our mind, our body is going to reveal that with negative mannerisms. If we have positive or good information in our brain, our body is going to expose those positive emotions. I often use the example of a puppy. We know that if the puppy has the tail tucked in between the legs, it is best to leave that puppy alone, but if the tail is up and wagging, the puppy is happy. In the same way, think of how many times we come across people or individuals who, when they walk into a room, we feel the negative vibes. Or vice versa, someone might walk in the room and we can tell right away they are happy. A similar thing happens when you speak to someone on the phone. Our voice can be a signal as to what is really going on inside our heads. Remember, the body reacts to how we think. As we progress through the pages of this book, we are going to learn about using awareness to be able to recognize negative thoughts and thinking patterns and then to take actions that are more aligned with what we are trying to do or achieve.

White Bear Theory

The ironic process theory, also known as the white bear theory, states that for you not to think about something, you have to think of the very same thing first. It refers to the psychological process, whereby, deliberate attempts to suppress certain thoughts make them more likely to surface in your mind. For example, if I said to you right now, do not think of a blue horse, you are likely to think of a blue horse. If, you don't want to think of a blue horse, you first think of a blue horse and then make a decision in your mind to think about something else. How many times have you shared a problem or situation with someone close to you and they told you not to think of it. According to this theory, that advice leads us or causes us to think about it even more. In the chapters to come, you are going to learn how to be in control of your thinking so you can deviate from negative thoughts and be in control of what you choose to think about.

Again, remember to come back to these principles and theories as often as you want to while you are reading this book. I often ask people, "How are you going to improve at something if you don't even know what you are looking to improve on?". Knowing and understanding what you are working towards is essential for your growth and development.

"Theory is splendid but
until put into practice,
it is valueless."
James Cash Penney

7 Steps to Becoming
The Best Version of Yourself

Step #1: Awareness

Step #2: Responsibility

Step #3: Communication

Step #4: Stress

Step #5: Relaxation

Step #6: Attitude

Step #7: Goals

Step #1

To Becoming
The Best Version of Yourself

AWARENESS

Awareness

"Life is like an egg.
When an external force breaks the egg, life ends.
When an internal force breaks the egg, life begins."
Jim Kwik

Ever since I retired from baseball, people will often ask me what would have been of my career if I knew all the things that I know now about the mind and mental strength. My answer is always the same: I have no idea. I can look back at my career as an athlete and I can tell you that I did practice a lot of the techniques you will read about in this book. However, I also consistently practiced some of the most detrimental ways to sabotage my thinking and my mentality. Early in 2009 I had the opportunity to work with Ken Ravizza. Ken was one of the best mental coaches of my era, and at that moment, I made the decision to blow him off. As ironic and funny as it seems now, I didn't believe in the mental side of the game. At that time, I didn't have the necessary awareness to realize I needed help, not just on the mental side of baseball but also on the mental side of life. That same year, after battling injuries, I started understanding the power of the mind, did my own research, and became so fascinated with the mind that I decided I wanted to help and lead people to use the power of the brain to their advantage. Sadly, I will never know the potential benefits to my baseball career if I had just allowed Ken to help me. I know the benefits of what working on myself has brought to my life after baseball, and because of that, I know it would have turned my baseball career around. But again, I will never know. That's the reason why I passionately work with anyone interested in bettering their life—athletes and non-athletes. My lack of awareness stopped me from working with one of the best ever. That damn awareness!

The definition of awareness is to have knowledge or perception of a situation or a fact. It means to be conscious of something. Being conscious, on the other hand, means to be aware of and to respond to one's surroundings. So, what is the difference between being aware and being conscious?

Even though both words seem to have the same meaning in language, they refer to remarkably different concepts. If you are anything like me, you may think of possible problems or situations that could happen and start thinking how you could get out of those situations. We have all seen a movie that made us think of the things we would do if we were in that specific situation. Let's use our imagination for a bit.

Imagine you are at the bank the moment the bank is being robbed. As the thieves come in the door, they order everyone to stay where they are, and raise their hands.

"Do not move," they shout. As you are standing there with your arms up high, your adrenaline starts to raise. Your mind starts to think of possible options or solutions. You become aware and start counting the thieves, what they are wearing, and things that stand out. You are even considering possible escape routes, playing the hero, or simply staying put and following what they say until the robbery is done. You are aware of a lot of the things that are happening, but you are also conscious about the possibility of something going bad and ending the journey of your life.

Being aware, fundamentally, has a physical-related expression. You are aware, for example, that your actions have consequences. You know that years of excessive drinking can lead to liver failure. You are aware that consuming too much sugar can lead to obesity, diabetes, and other diseases. You are aware of your realities, primarily because of factors like sensations, perceptions, cognitive abilities, and knowledge.

Being conscious is more like spirituality, where the physical world no longer obstructs your understanding. It is about being aware of the metaphysical world, about being concerned with the nature of existence, being, and the world. Aristotle referred to it as "wisdom," the subject of first causes and the principles of things.

Being conscious has a lot more depth than being aware and awareness is a prerequisite for consciousness. There is no way to be conscious about something if you are not aware of it first. With the example of the bank robbery, you were aware of everything in your surroundings, but you were consciously thinking about the worst thing that could happen.

Self-awareness is the ability to see yourself clearly and objectively through reflection and self-examination. It's the ability to focus on yourself and how your actions, thoughts, or emotions do or don't align with your internal standards.

Self-Awareness Theory

The self-awareness theory is based on the idea that you are not your thoughts, but that you are the entity observing your thoughts. You are the thinker, separate and apart from the thoughts you have. When we self-examine ourselves, we can give some thought to whether we are thinking, feeling, or acting according to our values and standards. In fact, we do this every day when we use our values and standards to judge how "correct" our thoughts and behaviors are.

There are two types of self-awareness; internal self-awareness and external self-awareness. Internal self-awareness represents how clearly we see our own selves, our thoughts, feelings, behaviors, and values as well as our passions, goals, strengths and weaknesses. External self-awareness represents how other people view us, in terms of the same factors mentioned above.

Research suggests that when we see ourselves clearly, we are less likely to cheat, lie, or steal because we make better decisions, communicate more effectively, and build stronger relationships. We are more creative and more confident in our abilities. In addition, research also suggests that practicing self-awareness can make us more proactive, boost our acceptance, and encourage self-development. It allows us to practice self-control and see things from the perspective of others.

Benefits of Self-Awareness

The benefits of self-awareness are a good enough reason to practice becoming more self-aware. You will discover more benefits as you become more in tune with yourself. Self-awareness is something you can learn and use anytime, and anywhere. It has the potential to enhance every experience you have, so that you live in the moment, evaluate yourself and the situation, and make better decisions.

Dr. Tasha Eurich, an organizational psychologist and researcher set on a quest to study self-awareness. The large-scale study of involving 10 separate investigations and nearly 5,000 participants revealed surprising roadblocks, myths and truths about self-awareness. The results concluded that although most people believe they are self-aware, only about 10-15% of the people studied met the criteria. Contrary to what most people believe, the research showed that we do not always learn from experience and that seeing ourselves as highly experienced can keep us from continuing to grow.

It is important to mention that improving our self-awareness through introspection or self-examination can be challenging because during the process of self-examination, we are likely to reflect on the causes of our own thoughts, feelings and behavior. Dr. Eurich's research discovered that people who practice introspection are actually less self-aware, not because it is ineffective, but because people are doing it incorrectly.

The Why Versus the What Question

The most common question during introspection or self-examination is the question 'why?' We often ask this question when trying to understand our emotions, behavior, and our attitudes. For example, you may have asked yourself the following question that deals with an emotion, why do I like person A more than person B? or this question that deals with a behavior, why did I lose my temper with X person? Or this last question that deals with an attitude, why am I upset about what X person did?

The most important consequence of asking ourselves the question 'why?' is that the answer leads us to a negative response. Why do I like person A more than person B? Because person A is fun and person B is always serious. Why did I lose my temper with that person? Because he/she was disrespectful. Why am I upset about what that person did? Because that person believes different things than I do.

The question 'why?' invites unproductive, and often negative thoughts to our mind. Ask yourself a "why" question and prove it to yourself. Why am I not liked? Why do I not have a job? Why can't I change? Why can't I perform well? Why can't I sleep? Why? Why? Why? What answers did you get? Research has shown that people who frequently analyze their own life with the question 'why?' are more depressed, anxious, and experience poor well-being. Why? Because people who are very introspective are more likely to get caught in repetitive, negative thinking patterns, or dwell on the negative answers.

To increase productive self-insight and decrease unproductive thoughts ask yourself 'what?' questions instead of 'why' questions. The question 'what?' leads to an action plan, it helps us stay objective, future-focused, and empowers us to act on our new insight. For example, what can I do to like person A as much as person B? What can I do to control my temper? What can I do to remain in control? Ask yourself a 'what' question and see the difference. What can I do to be more likable? What can I do to get a job? What can I do to change? What can I do to perform well? What can I do to sleep better?

A very common question I am often asked involves "what?" and "why?" questions. Almost every week I get calls, emails, and text messages about how to improve sleeping patterns. Every time, I ask people a very simple question. "Why can't you sleep?" The common answers I get are:

- There is too much stuff in my mind,
- I have too many things to do,
- My phone,
- The television,
- My roommate is loud,

- Music, etc.

I then follow up their answers with a second question. "In a perfect world, what can you do to get better sleep?" And frequent responses I get are:

- I could write whatever is on my mind on a piece of paper,
- I can write a list of the things I have to do,
- I can put my phone to charge far away from me,
- I can turn off the television and leave the remote control somewhere else,
- I can talk to my roommate and come to an agreement,
- I can turn the music off or wear earplugs, etc.

After the person has named a few things they can do to get better sleep, I often tell them to go ahead and do those things and see how their sleep improves.

Many times, I've been asked, "That's it?"

They are shocked at how easy it might be and I always respond, "Yes, that's it!"

As you can see, the difference between asking yourself one question versus another question is very powerful. The 'why?' question leads to negative answers and therefore, causes us to dwell on information. The 'what?' question leads us to create an action plan and all we have to do is follow the plan. It is not to say that following the plan is an easy thing to do. There may be some answers to the 'what' question that are going to be really difficult to follow, but in theory, it is that easy if we just do what we need to do.

Let's say for example you want to lose 10 pounds. Why do you want to lose ten pounds? Common answers are:

- I am unhappy with the way I look,

- My clothes don't fit anymore, or
- Simply stated, I am fat.

Well, what can you do to feel better and lose 10 pounds? Common answers are:

- I could eat healthier and better,
- I could start working out or going to the gym,
- I could create a routine, etc.

The reason I mentioned that it could be challenging to take action on following the plan is because change is difficult. When we want to change something, we are aware of the things we need to do, but we are also conscious about how challenging it is going to be. In the example mentioned above, how challenging it is to eat differently, work out, and start a new routine?

The 'why?' question is not always negative. It can be very power-ful and valuable when you ask the question correctly. For example, when you ask yourself, "Why you do what you do?" "Why you want to accomplish something?" Such questions are future-based and, therefore, bring up feelings, emotions, and sensations that are positive and bring motivation and passion.

People who practice both internal and external self-awareness, who seek honest feedback from loving critics, and who ask 'what?' instead of 'why?' can learn to see themselves more clearly. They also gain the rewards that increasing self-knowledge delivers. The beau-tiful thing about self-awareness is that no matter how much progress we make, we can always improve and learn more.

Replacing the 'why?' question with the 'what?' question will allow you to find solutions to the questions, doubts, and fears that enter your mind. It is about seeing beyond the problems and turning yourself into a problem-solving machine.

To improve our self-awareness, research suggest 5 things that we can do:

- Create time and space,
- Practice mindfulness,
- Journal your awareness,
- Practice listening, and
- Gain a different perspective.

Each one of these topics is going to be explained in detail in the coming chapters and each topic will provide a 'what to do' in order to improve.

One of the goals of this book is to help you gain awareness so that you can recognize the negativity that surrounds you. Negative thoughts and negative thinking patterns may be stopping you from achieving your maximum potential. Once you become aware, you can consciously decide to change the old negative patterns and turn them into positive thinking patterns. This way, you can start developing a new mentality.

Self-awareness leads us to being mindful or aware of our thoughts, which with practice and repetition is a skill that we can all learn.

*See appendix for questions to ask yourself and start to practice gaining more self-awareness.

Mindfulness

Mindfulness is going to be explained in more detail in the fifth Step to Becoming the Best Version of Yourself. But for now, I just want to give you a quick overview of what it is and how it works so that we can better understand the process of self-regulation.

The dictionary defines mindfulness as the quality or state of being conscious or aware of something. Mindfulness is about a special kind of attention characterized by an attitude of openness, curiosity, and acceptance. It is a mental state that is achieved by focusing one's awareness on the present moment, while calmly acknowledging and accepting one's feelings, thoughts, and body sensations. Mindfulness is a quality all human beings possess, it is not something that will just appear out of nowhere, it is something we can all learn to access through a process called self-regulation.

Self-Regulation

Self-regulation is about exercising and appreciating the ability you have to regain control of your emotions upon recognizing that you have unintentionally allowed them to control you. It is through self-regulation that we can gain more self-awareness.

A good strategy for self-regulation is to start with an anchor, as it is known in Neuro Linguistic Programming and Mindfulness. An anchor is a physical thing you can see, hear, smell, taste, or touch. An anchor sets up a stimulus response pattern so you can feel the way you want to, when you need to. Examples of anchors can be:

- A coin makes me feel strong,
- Jewelry makes me feel calm,
- A tattoo makes feel happy,
- Touching a knuckle makes me feel powerful,
- A pen gives me confidence, or
- A cup makes me feel energy, to name a few.

Once you have an anchor, and a feeling or emotion is attached to that anchor, begin to focus on your breathing. Then shift your focus to your anchor, which now has thoughts of feelings or emotions attached to it. Finally, redirect your attention to your breathing. This quick exercise will allow you to be more self-aware and will allow you to be more in control. An anchor can take your mentality from one place to another and allow you to feel how you want to feel. You can use it as much as you want, or as much as you need it. The key is to know that it is there for you to use when you want to use it. Be aware that not using the anchor over a period of time will cause the associated feelings and emotions to disappear. The idea of an anchor is to be used consistently to allow you to feel a specific way.

Belief Systems

A belief system of a person is the set of beliefs the person has about what is right and wrong and what is true and false. Your belief system, together with genetics, habits and personality is one of the strongest forces that affect the decisions you make.

To better understand where belief systems come from, it is important to dig a little into the nature versus nurture debate. When it comes to studying certain aspects of behavior, this debate argues the extent to which behaviors are inherited (genetics) or acquired (learned) influences. Belief systems fall under the nurture part of the debate. After conception, all humans start accumulating thousands and thousands of beliefs through what we hear, what we see on the news, what we read or any external influence we may be exposed to. All these beliefs that we accumulate throughout our lifetime interact with one another, affect one another, and together they form a system.

Belief systems are heavily influenced by our parents, culture, environment and therefore lead our thinking and our beliefs in a particular way. Our belief system creates perception, emotions, values, habits and our reactions to stimuli. The first seven years of one's life are the most important in developing the foundation of the belief system. It is during this time that a child's basic building blocks of perception is set. The belief system we develop as children will stick with us and drive our life into adulthood. After seven years of age, our subconscious mind can be reprogrammed by life experiences and through making different decisions we have the power to change and dictate the direction of our life.

Beliefs do not exist in isolation, rather, they interact and reinforce one another. If a set belief changes, other parts of the system will have to re-arrange in order to maintain the consistency of the system. A change in one belief affects the system as a whole.

Science has proven that is possible to change the perception of our beliefs and when we do, our brain sends different messages to our cells and reprograms itself. If you want to change your situation, you must alter your perception of your "reality" in your belief system. In all, to change the course of our life, you must change your belief system.

Think about some of the cultural beliefs you were raised with. How did those beliefs influence your life up until now? How did those beliefs influence your decision-making process? Have some of those beliefs changed?

As you continue to read this book, your subconscious mind is going to be reprogrammed with new information about your thinking patterns, about yourself, your attitude, your behavior, and the course you want for the rest of your life.

"At the center of your being
you have the answer
you know who you are
and you know what you want."
Lao Tzu

Exercise #1

Purpose: to gain awareness of your negativity and replace negative thoughts, with positive thinking patterns.

To really know what to do with this exercise it is important you understand the difference between thoughts and thinking. These are two very common words we use in our everyday language and yet most of us don't know what they mean or know the difference.

A thought, as defined in the dictionary, is an idea or opinion occurring suddenly in the mind. In common language, a thought is something that comes to your awareness or to your perceived reality. Thoughts can come from anywhere, and everywhere. Thoughts come into the mind through our five senses and we cannot control them. Anything we see, smell, taste, hear, or touch can put a new thought in your head. For example, as you are reading this, what if I put new thoughts in your head that you didn't want in your awareness? Like a pen, water, sunglasses, or any other word. You did not want those thoughts in your head, however, just by mentioning them, I put them there for you. A thought is like conditioning, we condition ourselves and our mind to the meaning of words that, when brought to awareness, are associated to a pervious stimulus.

On the other hand, thinking is the process of using one's mind to consider or reason about something. Thinking occurs when we choose to explore a thought and continue thinking about that specific thought. The beautiful thing is that we can actually control all of our thinking. We have free will, a sense of self, and awareness of our surroundings. We can choose to think about anything we want to think about. A study conducted by scientists David Oakley and Peter Halligan demonstrated that "the contents of consciousness are generated 'behind the scenes' by fast, efficient, non-conscious systems in our brain. All this happens without any interference from our personal awareness, which sit passively in the passenger seat while these processes occur." In short, we don't consciously choose our thoughts or our feelings—we become aware of them.

If we cannot control our thoughts but we can control what we think about, why do we continue to think in a negative way? According to the National Science Foundation, about 80% of our thoughts are negative or geared toward negativity. And considering our mind is connected to the body, as proven by the Chevreul's pendulum, the negativity we choose to think about is affecting our bodies. This exercise is about becoming aware of the negative thoughts that come into your mind and making a decision to change the negative thought for a positive thinking pattern. Remember, you can choose and decide what you think about, start thinking about positive things because your body is always listening. Whether you decide to think negatively or positively, your body will always be listening.

Thought replacement is about being aware of any negativity that comes into your mind and replacing it with positive thinking patterns. As you start doing this awareness exercise, you will realize just how negative our minds are. With the recognition of your negative thoughts, you can decide to think something positive.

Step #2

To Becoming
The Best Version of Yourself

RESPONSIBILITY

Responsibility

"You must take personal responsibility.
You cannot change the circumstances,
the seasons, or the wind,
but you can change yourself."
Jim Rohn

The human brain is an incredibly complex machine that constantly evolves. Each year, new information and discoveries about the power of our brain surface. This is really exciting, because we can continue to learn about the wonders of our brain and continue to use the brain's power to work on self-improvement.

Responsibility is one of my favorite topics to talk about because of the complexities that we face when we put the word into action. The most important aspect of taking responsibility for your life is to admit and understand that your life is your responsibility. No one else can live your life for you. You make the decisions. You are in charge. You are in control.

But are we really in control? Are we truly responsible?

I want to share these topics, as well as the solutions, early in the book so that you can be more responsible about how you think, about the decisions you make, and about how you live your life. Being responsible will allow your mind to rest at night because you have owned up to your decisions and taken responsibility. In all, it will lead you to a more peaceful life. Being responsible goes hand-in-hand with the thought replacement exercise, as being responsible is one of the most positive things you can do.

Most of us have an idea of what responsibility is and often associate it with being accountable. A responsible person accepts the consequences of his or her actions and decisions. It can lead you to be more honest, more independent, and more reliable. Through responsibility you create the principles and morals that lead your life. That is the reason why responsibility requires effort and commitment. Today, responsibility is highly valued because it brings security, confidence and stability.

What I want to do is introduce you to another definition of the word responsibility, which can also be described as the ability to act independently and make decisions without authorization. Being responsible is an ability, which means that it can be learned and improved. If, up to this point, you have not been responsible enough in your life, it is my hope that you take charge so that you can start becoming the person you want to be. Becoming the best version of yourself is going to require you to be extremely responsible. Based on the definition above, to act independently means to do things on your own, to take charge, and take care of your part. To make decisions without authorization means that you are equipped to make the best possible decision and will take full responsibility for the outcome, regardless of what the outcome is. That is not to say you cannot do research, ask friends, family members, or your mentors. It is about gathering as much information as possible and equipping yourself with information to make the best possible decision. I personally know and understand how difficult this process can be, but also know how amazing it is to not have to look over your shoulder because you are being responsible and making the best decision you can make.

Being responsible encompasses many areas of life such as:

- Doing the right thing,
- Telling the truth,
- Being on time,
- Taking care of yourself,
- Doing your chores,
- Taking care of your kids, and
- Teaching the right things, etc.

You name it, a lot of the things we do in our daily life can fall under this incredible topic of responsibility. Nonetheless, the real question is, are you being responsible? Can you genuinely look at your life and say you are being responsible in all areas of your life? I doubt it, but that's the beauty about life, we can always improve, and now, you can start to live your life responsibly.

I'd like to share with you some of the benefits that being a responsible person can bring to your life, so that as you are working on your transformation, you can see the value behind this amazing word. Being responsible leads to being respected because everyone respects someone who is truthful. It can lead you to have more confidence because when you see each situation as a learning experience, you are confident that you can improve and, therefore, continue to build confidence in yourself. Being responsible can help you solve more problems. When you are conscious to consider your own mistakes, you are more likely to find the solutions to the problems. In addition, you are likely to experience better relationships because accepting responsibility shows humility, empathy and compassion. Being responsible will also improve your decision-making process as you will be in control of yourself to take-action, and by acting, you are being responsible. Lastly, being responsible will lead you to become a role model for others around you, where your life and the way you live is a testament of what is like to be a true leader who lives a responsible life. All these areas or opportunities for learning and growth, are topics you will work on as you continue to read this book.

Furthermore, I want to note that being responsible or taking responsibility can be a daring thing to do. It can be scary. It can be frightening. Taking responsibility can cause a lot of pain and hurt. Personally, I know that feeling too-well because I too, lived irresponsibly. I understand the feeling of the adrenaline rushing through the body when it is time to face the consequences. Years ago, I chose to come clean and to face the consequences for the poor decisions I had made. After all, I made those mistakes in the first place, so in my mind, it was the right thing to do; to come clean and be responsible for my actions—be responsible for me. I am, by no means, insinuating you have to or should do the same and come clean for your faults and mistakes. The point I am trying to make is, to say I am responsible for me, for my actions, and my decisions and you are responsible for yours. Only you know, deep in your mind, what you can do and what you should do. I speak for myself and let me assure you that although the consequences for taking responsibility can be enormous, when I took responsibility for my actions, a huge weight was lifted off my shoulders. Now, I can genuinely say I am at peace. Today, I live my life with the awareness of making better decisions and living responsibly so that I don't put myself in those situations again.

Many times, to accept a fault or a mistake, or to accept that we have done something wrong can be seen as a weakness, but it is the complete opposite; it is a sign of supreme confidence and respect.

We, as humans, aren't perfect and never will be. We make mistakes, we sin, we fail, and we are weak, but we are all also the opposite. We can correct mistakes; we can live being aware and wanting to do the right thing. We can strive to be successful and can be as strong as we want to be. It is all a personal decision. Being responsible or being irresponsible is also a personal decision. You get to make that decision on your own. Just remember that what we repeatedly do, becomes a habit. It is completely up to you to live the way you want to live, but if you truly want to become a master of your mind, you must start by taking responsibility for your actions and becoming a responsible person as a whole.

There is a famous quote by Aristotle that says, "We are what we repeatedly do. Excellence, therefore, is not an act, but a habit." What I am suggesting is that you start developing the habit of being responsible.

Habits

Humans are creatures of habit. We learn by repetition, from the words we use to the behaviors we exert, and a lot of other things in between. Whether you realize it or not, our daily behavior is made up of habits; automatic behaviors that we do without thinking. In sports, for example, we work over and over on one specific drill to improve our physical skills. We do the same in our lives, we do the same things over and over and we become better at our habits. If you think about it, you have dozens, if not hundreds of habits that you have developed over time. Our mentality works the same way, it creates patterns and ways of thinking that become habitual. We think and act in certain ways out of habit. The good news is that we can replace our bad habits or the habits we don't like with new positive habits or habits we want. But before we move into changing habits, I want to make sure you understand how important and essential habits are in our life.

Habits are necessary in our everyday life. We go through most of our days engaging in good habits, routines, and activities. If we didn't, we would have to think about everything single thing we do, which would require a lot of energy and effort. Professor Russell Poldrack from Stanford University explains that "habits are an adaptive feature of how the brain works and we want the brain to learn how to do things without energy and effort." Many habits involve the release of dopamine, a feel-good chemical or reward in our brain. When we engage in a new 'rewarding' behavior we feel excited from doing it because of the dopamine release. This is one of the reasons why we form bad habits in the first place.

According to a 2010 study published in The European Journal of Social Psychology, it takes an average of 66 days for a behavior to change, though time varied from 18 to 254 days. When replacing or creating a new habit, understand that the time it takes to develop or change, may be different for everyone. Likewise, remember that habits are learned through repetition. Stay encouraged and motivated and keep in mind that if the change is good for you, then it is worth to put the energy, time and effort.

Since habits form through practice and repetition, the same is true for breaking habits. The following are five strategies recommended by scientists to eliminate and form new habits.

- Lower your stress levels,
- Know your cues,
- Replace a bad habit with a good one,
- Have a better reason for quitting, and

- Set better goals.

In steps 4 and 5, we are going to learn about stress and relaxation so you can reduce your stress levels. Knowing your cues or triggers can help you avoid them in the first place through awareness. Replacing bad habits with new ones is like thought replacement. It is about changing a negative habit for a new positive one. If, for example, you have the habit of smoking, every time a thought about smoking comes into your mind, replace it with chewing gum or another positive thinking pattern. Having a better reason for quitting has to do with communication and how we communicate with ourselves, which we are going to talk about in more depth in the following step. Lastly setting better goals is going to be explained in detail in the 7th Step to Becoming the Best Version of Yourself.

According to researchers, about 40% of our behaviors on any given day are attributed to our habits. Your life today is basically a compilation of your habits. The minute you start to change your bad habits for good habits, you will begin to transform your life.

Routines

Optimizing our daily life can help us get on top of our game and one of the best things we can do to enhance our life is to have a routine. It may sound counter-intuitive but developing a daily routine can benefit our mental health as routines can help us to feel more in control of our life. All of us have routines, things that we do day in and day out as a habit. Today, most of us are accustomed to living our lives in a hurry, moving from one thing to another or from one place to another. We are often on the go. A lot of the things we do in our everyday life are part of a routine.

Our lives are unpredictable and can often be anxiety provoking. Routines are something that we know we do well, and we are comfortable doing, which can serve as an anchor of predictability and lower anxiety levels. Routines can also help us cope with change, form healthy habits, and reduce tension and stress.

As previously mentioned, an anchor sets up a stimulus response pattern so you can feel the way you want to, when you need to. A routine can serve the purpose of an anchor because no matter what we are going through in life it is always comforting to know we are going to be doing something we know we do well. For example, knowing you are going to eat dinner around a certain time every day, or going to bed around the same time everyday can produce a feeling of comfort and satisfaction. Routines become part of who we are and what we do, just like habits, and can greatly help us reduce tension and stress levels. It is of extreme importance to set mental health routines just as we do with the routines we create for our physical body. Dr. Steve Orma mentions that to manage anxiety, "You need to consistently check in with yourself about what you are worrying about, then address it. One way to do this is scheduling 'thinking time' to think through any problems or worries weighing on you instead of letting them build up." Orma adds that routines also help with stress: "Creating a set schedule for doing chores, work tasks, meetings, exercise, playing bills and all the usual things you need to do. Put these into your schedule. Once this becomes your normal routine, it's easier to accomplish everything because it becomes a habit."

The bottom line is that we all have routines even if we don't think we have one. We do certain things the same way each day. If you pay attention, and are aware of how you live your life, you will realize what some of your routines are. Once you realize your routine, you can change it or adapt it to your needs so that you can accomplish what you want to accomplish. If you don't have a routine, now is the time to start building a routine that can help you achieve your daily goals, and that can create the pave way to your long-term goals. Remember, we learn through repetition and before you know it, your routine will become a habit and you will do it without thinking about it.

Once you have your routine in place, it is important to consistently revisit or pay attention to what you are doing. Routines are very comforting to our bodies and often it's because of that same comfort that it is easy to deviate from the things that are working for us. For example, in my routine I know how important it is for me to practice a relaxation technique every day. However, life may get busy for a few days, and before I realize, I am living my life without relaxing, which often leads me to feel stressed and overwhelmed. Because my mind may be cluttered with information, tension and stress, I may not have the clarity of thinking that I need to be in control of my own mind. Sometimes it takes someone we know to reminds us of what we might need to do to get back on track. Nevertheless, keep in mind it is not anyone else's responsibility to take care of you; it is your own responsibility. Thus, be aware and constantly pay attention to your routine so that it makes you feel the way you want to feel. Make sure the things you want as part of your routine are always a part of your life. I know and understand that we all forget things from time to time but be aware and keep in mind that it is your responsibility to remember. So what can we do to remember? And how do we not forget what is important to us? We can find a way to remind ourselves the things that are important to us.

Reminders

The brain has an incredible capacity to store information, in fact scientists have discovered that our brain has the capacity to store ten times more information than we thought—an astonishing 4.7 billion books. But why do we forget things? We live in a world that is surrounded by information and technology, and our brains are constantly filling up with information. We are constantly saturating our brains with information that does not allow the brain to do what it is supposed to do—to think. When we forget things, or information, we are not being responsible. Forgetting things can have both, minor and serious consequences.

Think about how often you forget something important? You may forget an important date, a name, or words you want to use. Elizabeth Loftus, one of today's best-known memory researchers points out four major reasons why people forget:

- Retrieval failure,
- interference,
- failure to store, and
- motivated forgetting.

Retrieval failure is one of the most common causes of forgetting and it occurs when information vanishes from your memory like when you know the information is there, but you just can't remember it. The decay theory suggests that over time, if information is not retrieved and rehearsed, the memory traces begin to fade, and it will eventually be lost. Interference refers to the idea that memories compete and interfere with other memories and it happens in two different ways: proactively and retroactively. Proactive interference happens when an old memory makes it difficult to remember a new memory and retroactive interference happens when new information interferes with previously learned information. Failure to store refers to the idea that the information we want to remember never made it into the long term-memory. Lastly, motivated forgetting occurs when we actively work to forget memories such as traumatic or disturbing experiences.

Forgetting is not something we can avoid; however, it is something we can work on to improve by putting strategies into practice and therefore, be more responsible.

As previously mentioned, we live in a world surrounded by technology and the number one example is our phone. According to GMSA real-time data, as to the date of this book's publishing, 5.28 billion people have a mobile device, that is 67.95% of the world's population. Most of our phones have some type of alarm system that we can use as a tool to help us remember information. I often share with my clients my phone and the incredible number of alarms I have set on my phone. I share this with them because I, too, forget information. The alarms on my phone continuously remind me of the things I have to do or the things I want to get done. For example, I have a daily alarm set at 2:20pm. My kids get out of school at 2:25pm so when the alarm goes off, I know it is time for me get in the car and go pick them up. People often ask me if I really forget to pick up my kids, which I don't. However, I may be busy or occupied doing something else, like cooking, working, or I might simply be distracted. The alarm is just a reminder to let me know that I have something going on when it goes off.

Alarms are a great tool to help us remember things we have to or want to do. If you can get in the habit of creating alarms for the different things you have to do throughout the day, it will remind you of what you want to get done. A physical calendar is also another great tool that I talk to all my clients about. When you have the tasks and activities you have to do (or want to do) written down, it makes it more likely for you to constantly revisit the calendar. Lastly, I tell people to invest in Post-its. Post-it notes serve as a great reminder because you can post them anywhere you want, and you will constantly be looking at the information you wrote down in them. The idea is simple but powerful. If our brain is going to forget information, why not help ourselves to remember that information through a variety of tools such as alarms, calendar, and Post-its? It is your responsibility to remember what you need to get done or what you want to accomplish, so I encourage you to use these tools to help your brain remember information. Always look to improve yourself one way or another.

Kaizen

The beginnings of Kaizen trace back to World War II where multiple experts collaborated and created tools that eventually became what is now known as Kaizen. After WWII, the nation of Japan was greatly impacted and damaged by the war. During the rebuilding process, Japan started to develop management concepts with the idea of improvement.

The word Kaizen is a composed word made up of two different words. There's Kai, which represents change, and the word Zen, which represents good. The literal translation would be "change, good." In English, the term implies implementing continuous improvement. The Kaizen method is a very common practice in Japan and is the base model for quality improvement in areas such as:

- Suggestion,
- Systems,

- Small groups,
- Zero defects,
- Production,
- Maintenance,
- Automation,
- Total quality control etc.

Today, Kaizen is recognized worldwide as an important pillar of an organization's long-term competitive strategy. In the words of Masaaki Imai, Founder of the Kaizen Institute, "Kaizen means improvement. Moreover, it means continuing improvement in personal life, home life, social life, and working life."

Improvement is not just about making something better, it is about the genuine good of the people or the process. To improve or create change, we must devote ourselves to create new habits and we must have self-discipline to follow through to create the change.

Kaizen is more than a word and more than a concept, it is a way of life. As Masaaki Imai says, it is about "improving the world with everyone, everywhere, every day." Years ago, I became fascinated with this term and the meaning behind Kaizen and started applying all these managerial concepts into my own life. I remember asking myself what would happen if I applied this concept or philosophy to my life. To continuously improve the overall well-being of my life in every possible area such as:

- My personality,
- My behavior,
- My attitude,
- My decision making,
- My mentality,
- My education,

- My parenting, etc.

…and so I began my journey.

I started living the Kaizen way and put my energy, my attention, and my focus on the overall improvement of my entire life. It is my wish that you can examine your own life for areas of improvement. It doesn't matter how little or how big the improvement is because any improvement is better than no improvement at all. I hope that moving forward you start to take action to improve in all areas of your life. Seeing changes and improvements in your life will encourage you and motivate you to continue to move forward with a positive outlook. Living out the changes is rewarding beyond words and striving to become the best version of yourself is incredibly satisfying.

Learn and Share

One of the most important qualities of leadership is the act of moving people toward a common goal that makes them better. In this section, I want to encourage you to share with others the wealth of information you are learning. Look for ways to pass on your knowledge to other people around you. Knowledge is power, but knowledge without application is useless. Napoleon Hill once said that, "knowledge has no value except that which can be gained from its application towards a worthy end." I believe it's a part of our responsibility as mentally strong and responsible individuals to empower others around us so that they too can improve their lives.

"Leadership is making others better
as a result of your presence and
making sure that impact lasts in your absence."
Harvard Business School

Exercise #2

Purpose: to be responsible and eliminate blaming, complaining, and making excuses.

Taking responsibility can be a challenging thing to do for many reasons. For many of us, it is very difficult to see ourselves as being bad, and therefore we create illusions in our mind about our reality. We do what we have to do to justify ourselves. We justify our mind, our behavior, our attitude, and our actions. It is often much simpler to blame, to complain, and to make an excuse than it is to take responsibility. Blaming is to assign responsibility to something or someone else, whereas complaining is a verbal expression of unhappiness, displeasure, frustration, or discontentment. An excuse is an explanation used to justify an offense, fault or mistake.

In general, most of us are very good at using or doing one of the three things mentioned above. Many times, we do these things without conscious awareness, meaning we do them without thinking, as a habit. Through awareness, and by paying attention to how you think and what you are thinking, you are to eliminate blaming, complaining, and making excuses from your day to day life. This exercise is about paying attention to your thoughts and thinking patterns to identify moments in which you are likely to blame, complain, or make an excuse. Once you are aware, immediately replace that thought with a positive thinking pattern and assume responsibility.

Step #3

To Becoming
The Best Version of Yourself

COMMUNICATION

Communication

"The quality of your communication
is the quality of your life."
Tony Robbins

Throughout history, all animal species have found a way to use a system of communication to survive and evolve. It is through communication that we can learn, understand, and interpret the world around us. It is through our ability to communicate that we make our way through the world and through our life. In fact, researchers believe it would be impossible to live without communication or the ability to communicate.

Some of the oldest forms of communication include talking or making sounds, drawing, painting, dancing, acting, and using symbols. The first species of man, the homo sapiens, appeared around 130,000 BC. However, it wasn't until around 30,000 BC that communication began to take place on an intentional manufactured format. The homo sapiens used animal blood, colored minerals, and pigments made from the juice of fruits and berries to create the first paintings ever found on caves. The depiction of primitive life on the cave walls has puzzled scholars for years but it is believed that these paintings were used as a manual for instructing others. Fast forward to 3500 BC and the first cuneiform writing was developed by the Sumerians, while the Egyptians developed what is known as hieroglyphic writing. Today, as we continue to grow and develop as human beings, our communication seems to have hit a plateau and we are not communicating effectively with others, and/or others are not communicating effectively with us. The bottom line is, we are not very good communicators and communication alone accounts for a large part of the tension and stress in our minds. Bettering the communication with ourselves and others will lead us to live a more fulfilling, stress-free, and satisfying life.

Understanding Communication

I've always been fascinated by how certain things we think we know may not necessarily be true. Most of us take for granted the real meaning of words and at times, we use words without truly knowing their meaning. Up until 2012, I thought I knew what the word *communication* meant. It turns out that this word appears in the business dictionary twice. I was intrigued. Two different meanings for a word that most of us believe we know the meaning to. The business dictionary has a definition for the word communication and a similar but very different definition for the word effective communication.

Communication is a two-way process of reaching mutual understanding in which participants not only exchange (encode and decode) information, news, ideas and feelings, but also create and share meaning. Effective communication is a two-way information sharing process that involves one party sending a message that is easily understood by the receiving party. The key difference between these two definitions are the words "easily understood." Effective communication requires a clear understanding from the receiving

party, which can be a difficult thing to achieve as several characteristics are involved when the communication process occurs.

The characteristics involved in the communication process are
individual to each person since each person has a different language,
culture, and personality. Education, past experiences, and goals are
also involved during the communication process. When a person
communicates with another, the sender is communicating a coded
message that the receiving person must de-code to clearly understand
the intended message. When communicating, both the sender and
the receiver have their own characteristics in play, which can lead to
the intended message to be easily misunderstood or misinterpreted.
Based on the individual characteristics of each person, some potential
problems can include:

- Incongruence,
- Too much information,
- The message might not be clear enough, and
- The information may be too long, or too difficult to understand.

Nonetheless, if we add and understand Albert Mehribian's
research on personal communication to the communication process,
we are more likely to find ourselves confused by the information we
are trying to de-code.

In 1967, Albert Mehribian's studies and research concluded that
we deduce our feelings, attitudes, and beliefs about what someone
says based on the speaker's body language and tone of voice and not
merely by words alone. Personal communication, according to the
findings of the study, showed that humans pay attention to words 7%
of the time, tone and voice 38% of the time, and body language 55%
of the time. Words are very powerful and have the influence to build
up a person or destroy a person internally. However, if scientifically

we listen to the actual spoken words just 7% of the time, and 38% to the tone and pitch, and we are not using the correct words, we are likely easily to run into problems when communicating.

Sure, we all think we know how to communicate, as it is something we do every single day, but is our communication clear and easily understood? According to a 20-year research at the University of Chicago, information is misunderstood or misinterpreted 46% of the times. That means that there is almost a 1 in 2 chance that whatever information you are trying to communicate is going to be misinterpreted or misunderstood. That is a scary reality. I have had the opportunity to talk many different groups of people, to groups from a few individuals to hundreds and thousands of people and it always amazes me to know that half of the listening audience have absolutely no idea what I am talking about or what I am saying; they are simply distracted or thinking of something else. They are physically there, but mentally, they are somewhere else. Think about when you are speaking to others, or you are listening to someone speak, isn't it amazing how easily information is misinterpreted or misunderstood?

The effective communication process looks intimidating at first glance, but it is quite simple if we just practice it regularly. It requires a sender, the person initiating the communication process, and a receiver, the person receiving the message. Both the sender and the receiver are highly influenced by past experiences, attitudes, skills, knowledge, perceptions, and culture, and therefore their interpretation of a message depends on what each individual person is going through in their own minds. Information is subject to interpretation and that is why it is important to know and understand the four steps for effective communication—encoding, medium of transmission, decoding, and feedback. Let me translate this for you. A sender is going to think about what they want to say and put it into words. As the sender is putting thoughts into words the sender is also thinking about how to communicate the message to the receiver, which could be face to face, text message, email, video, etc. As the message is sent, the receiver's job now is to interpret the message that was sent in his or her own way. Lastly, the receiver is to provide some feedback related to the message or the information to make sure everyone is on the same page. Sounds pretty simple if you asked me, however most of us fail at communicating effectively. We fail not just because we don't explain ourselves right, but also because we don't know exactly what's going on in the receiver's mind. The receiver might have problems or stress that he or she may be dealing with, or simply, because we don't know whether or not they are paying attention. The fourth and last step, the feedback process is where most of us fail to accomplish correctly, and the step that most humans skip when communicating. We tend to send or receive messages and we respond with a short answer—typically an okay, a smile, a thumbs up, or now days, we respond with an emoji. Nonetheless, we are completely unaware of whether the other person received the message the way we intended it to be. Without feedback the sender cannot confirm that the information was received correctly and is not given the chance to take corrective action in case there was misunderstanding or misinterpretation.

One of the most important keys to communicating effectively is to listen. It is of extreme importance to listen with the intent of under-standing and not to listen with the intent of responding. According to a study, we spend about 45% of our waking time listening and the same study revealed that most of us are poor listeners. Therefore, when listening, it is important to control your thinking patterns and your mind so that you can understand the information or the message that is being delivered to you. Then, take your time to respond with the best possible words depending on who you are speaking to. Avoid responding with the first thing that comes to mind, take the time to analyze, process the information, and focus on the meaning of what you want to communicate so that you can respond as clearly as possible.

In the Theories section of this book, I discussed the importance of personality assessments as an incredible tool to communicating more effectively. Myers Briggs Type Indicator is a phenomenal tool the improve the communication process and to develop rapport with others. Building rapport is crucial as it helps to build common ground and develop trust. Understanding human differences is an important step to take when communicating with other people. We are all different, we all think differently, and we all have different ideas and beliefs. Therefore, we all interpret information in our very own way.

Having rapport can be extremely beneficial not only to communicate more effectively but in life in general. Rapport establishes strong two-way connections and contrary to popular belief, rapport is a skill that can be learned. Rapport is the sense of connection or bond you establish with someone where mutual attentiveness, positivity and coordination occur. The best method to building strong rapport is the match and mirror technique. Behavioral research shows that copying other people's body language, mannerisms and repeating the words they use helps build trust and therefore establishes rapport. Matching and mirroring can effectively be done with respect and discretion and when done correctly, it creates positive feelings and responsiveness within one another. Matching and mirroring the most unconscious elements of a person's behavior, such as physiology and tonality accounts for an estimated 93% of our communication and if you discretely match words as well, the remainder 7%, you'd be matching and mirroring 100% of the personal communication model by Dr. Albert Mehribian.

Importance of Effective Communication

Various studies point out that the average human being spends 70 to 80% of their waking hours in some type of communication. Stop and think about it for a second. From the minute you wake up you are, in one way or another, engaged in some type of communication. You are involved in a type of communication by:

- Talking,
- Reading something on your phone,
- Checking up on social media,
- Watching television, or
- Listening to music etc.

You are constantly communicating and being informed about things all day long. But are we sending and receiving the messages as they were intended to be?

Being able to communicate effectively is perhaps the most important of all life skills. According to the Carnegie Institute of Technology, 85% of our success in life is directly attributed to communication skills. Only 15% is attributed to technical skills. It doesn't matter how knowledgeable, committed, prepared, ambitious, or educated you are, without good communication skills you are less likely to succeed.

Most of us think about communication as something that is instinctive. We rarely ever take the time to work on it because it is something we have always done. Not only this, but most of us believe we are good or excellent communicators when, in reality, it is the complete opposite. To illustrate, think about all of the times when you got into arguments because someone thought you said something you didn't. It has happened to all of us, and if we don't work on it, it will continue to happen in different areas our of life and could potentially cause problems at home, school, work, and our relationships. Developing good communication skills can be extremely valuable in every aspect of your life. It can:

- Strengthen relationships,
- Deepen connections,
- Build greater respect and trust,
- Improve problem-solving skills,
- Minimize tension and stress, and
- Improve your overall social and emotional health.

For most of us, however, communicating more clearly and effectively requires some extra learning. Learning the different ways in which we communicate and how each way of communication can potentially lead to misunderstanding and misinterpretation, will help you understand and recognize the very same things you can change and improve on. Although there are many different forms of communication, the four most common ways are the verbal, non-verbal, written, and visual.

As we previously learned, verbal miscommunication can occur very easily as there are several factors that influence each and every person's interpretation of a message. Each person's style of communication, beliefs, values, culture and other factors may influence miscommunication. Experts agree that a substantial portion of our everyday communication is non-verbal, meaning that we communicate through facial expressions, signs, gestures, and body language. Non-verbal details in communication reveal who we are and often impact how we relate to others and how others relate to us. In fact, it is said that non-verbal communication is more truthful that the spoken word. Think about it. Gestures, involuntary body movements, posture, eye gazing, appearance, artifacts, and even human touch are all forms of non-verbal communication. Any of these non-verbal elements can be misinterpreted. Written and visual communication work the same way and can also be misunderstood or misinterpreted very easily. Think about when you read a magazine, text messages, or when you watch a movie or look at pictures. We all interpret what we read or what we see in our very own way.

According to the Dynamic Signal Study, 80% of people feel stressed about ineffective communication. There's no surprise here. Communication is subject to personal interpretation and if we don't communicate effectively and double-check the feedback we receive, we are likely to create stress or feel stressed.

According to research the 4 most common things stopping us from communicating effectively are:

- Stress and out of control emotions,
- Lack of focus,
- Inconsistent body language, and
- Negative body language.

In the next step to Becoming the Best Version of Yourself, we are going to dive deeper into stress and stressors. In addition, in step number 6, we will discuss how to deal with emotions. Our lack of focus comes to us through the many different distractions we face daily. We often try to multi-task, we check our phone too much, or plan what we are going to say next in a conversation without taking the time to listen. We also daydream, and deal with a lot of noise either in the environment, or in our heads. Any of the things mentioned above can distract us and lead us to misinterpret information. Inconsistent body language refers to making sure that your body language is in sync with what you are communicating. For example, you can't say 'yes' while you are shaking your head. If you say one thing, and your body is representing or saying something else, it will send the wrong message to the listener. Negative body language is very much like inconsistent body language, many times when we disagree with something being said, we refuse the person's message by avoiding eye contact, crossing our arms, or moving our body in a specific way. It is not about agreeing with everything that it is being said, it is about being respectful of someone else's opinion and about avoiding sending negative signals.

How to Communicate Effectively

During my time as the mental skills Coordinator of the Kansas City Royals, we would have daily meetings with the coaches. During the meetings, coaches would find out about what was going on, and what we were doing that day. Also, there were medical updates, drills to be performed that day, times, etc. First thing in the morning, the schedule would be posted all over the complex for players, coaches, and staff to see. After the meeting, we would start our day, head down to the field and have a meeting with all the players about the work for the day. The information was communicated to the players and personnel visually, in writing, and vocally. It was amazing to see the confusion and misinterpretation of information that happened throughout the day every single day. It's just a good example of how it doesn't matter how well we think we are communicating, information can always be misinterpreted or misunderstood.

Communicating effectively is more about listening and less about talking. It is about personal responsibility to understand and be understood.

You can't listen correctly if you are constantly being distracted by other things, including your own thoughts and thinking patterns. Focus on the speaker and what they are saying. If you find it difficult to concentrate, try repeating the words you are hearing in your head. The repetition helps reinforce their message and helps you stay more focused.

Set aside judgements and avoid interrupting or trying to redirect the conversation. To communicate effectively you don't have to like someone, or their values, ideas, and opinions. However, you can be professional and set aside your judgement and withhold criticism and blame. In the same manner, you cannot concentrate if you are always planning what you are going to say next. You have to listen with the intent to understand and once the other person has finished talking, reflect on what was said and respond with what the information meant to you.

Pay attention to nonverbal signs. Sometimes the way you look, listen, move and react tell more about how you are feeling than words alone. Developing the ability to understand and use nonverbal cues in a positive way can help you:

- Connect better with others,
- Navigate difficult situations,
- Express what you really mean, and
- Build better and stronger relationships.

Be aware of cultural differences amongst people and understand that people from different countries and areas of the world use different nonverbal communication gestures.

Be an active listener. There is a difference between hearing and listening. When you listen, you are engaged in what is being said. Listening can also help lower stress levels and support physical and emotional well-being. If for example, the person you are talking to is calm, and you are truly listening, they will project that calmness onto you and therefore you will be calm. In the same manner, if a person is agitated or upset, you can help the person calm down by listening in an attentive way and making the person feel understood.

Always keep your stress in check. It is of extreme importance to recognize when stress is escalating so that we can quickly bring down our emotional intensity. Being in control of your thinking patterns and what you are thinking is key. It is about being in control of the mind and not letting the mind be in control of you. When you realize feelings and emotions are rising take a moment to calm down so you can regulate your feelings and emotions and behave appropriately.

Be flexible in your mind. Understand that people have different concepts, ideas and beliefs, and that not everyone thinks like you. Enjoy conversations and use humor to keep things loose and fun.

Lastly, as with most of the things we do, practice makes better, but excellent practice makes amazing. Practice having good communication skills and communicating effectively, and you will be more likely to achieve the success you want in life.

Asking Questions

During all my sessions, speaking engagements, presentations, and talks I often ask a simple question, "Do you have any questions?"

Most the time there is a profound silence and heads turning around to other people as to see if someone is going to ask a question. It is almost as if it was a scary and terrifying moment. Most of the time, I laugh internally because I know there is at least one person with a question, but they are too timid or too scared to ask. Later, people approach me with questions, or I am being asked questions through social media or my personal phone.

Have you ever felt dumb or stupid about asking a question? Asking questions carries an immense power because you are likely to get answers that have valuable information for personal and professional success. In a study at Harvard Business School the most prominent reason to people's reluctance to asking questions was because of fear of getting a negative evaluation. Even when information is not clear or we have doubts about what is being said, most of the time, we are reluctant or fearful to ask questions.

Albert Einstein, one of the most prominent scientists of our time, said, "I have no special talent. I am only passionately curious." Wisdom starts with knowledge, and knowledge starts with curiosity. Think for instance, of a child and the number of questions they ask. Children ask an innumerable number of questions because they don't know, they are curious, and it is by asking questions that they learn more about the world.

It is okay to not know something. There is no such thing as a stupid question, in fact, asking questions is not about how much you know. It is about learning, clarity and direction. Think about how much time, energy, and space you waste when you don't know something? Think about the tension and stress that comes from not knowing what to do or what direction to follow? Asking a question can give you the answer you need so you can focus on the task at hand and get things done. Every question has value, even the so-called stupid or dumb questions. It is the only way to learn and ensure you are on the right track. Asking questions is about learning in the process. What is easy for you doesn't mean it is easy for other people, some things that are obvious to you, may not be obvious to other people.

We have all been in a conversation, meeting, or lecture and felt completely lost. You have no idea what is going on and you have questions but are afraid of feeling dumb or stupid. Then someone else asks the same question you had, and you breathe a sigh of relief. But what if someone else had not asked the question? You and other people would have remained lost. A good way of looking at asking questions is to assume there are other people in the room who also don't know the answer to your question, and just ask it. If you are curious about something, chances are someone else is curious too.

Lastly, remember that you don't know it all. No matter how educated or knowledgeable you are, there are things you don't know about and the only way to learn is to ask questions. When you ask questions you:

- Discover something new,
- You put things together,
- You remember things,
- You resolve issues, and
- You understand people better.

One of the best ways to get answers you are looking for is to involve the 5 W's and the H. Ask:

- Who?
- What?
- When?
- Where?
- Why? and
- How?

Get the information and clarity you need and remember, the person asking the questions is always in control—and always keep in mind the ancient Chinese proverb, "He who asks questions remains a fool for 5 minutes. He who does not ask, remains a fool forever." Ask, ask, ask!

Self-Talk

Take a minute to think about how you talked to yourself today? If someone else, your best friend for example, talked to you the way you talk to yourself every day, would that person still be your best friend? It is an interesting question when put in a different perspective right?

Simply stated, self-talk is your internal dialogue which is influenced by your subconscious mind. It reveals thoughts, beliefs, questions, and ideas that you have. Internal communication can be both negative and positive and it can be detrimental or encouraging—it is up to you. Self-talk influences how you feel about yourself and how you respond to different events in your life.

It is said that the average person has thousands of internal conversations every single day—that is anywhere between 50,000 and 70,000 thoughts or thinking patterns per day. Behavioral research by The National Science Foundation demonstrates that 80% of our internal conversations or thoughts are negative or tend to be geared towards negativity. When you understand through the Chevreul's pendulum that your mind is connected to your body and that what you think about your body responds to, these numbers and stats are a sad and scary reality. Think about it, if your mind is connected to your body and most the things in your mind are negative, then your mind and body are negative.

A false truth is an invalid statement that for some reason was already perceived or assumed to be truth. It is very similar to the self-fulfilling prophecy, which states that a prediction causes itself to become true due to the behavior and expectation of the believer. A false truth influences our internal beliefs. Internal beliefs are the set of principles that help you interpret your everyday reality. Internal beliefs shape your personality and your behavior, and what's more interesting is that some of your internal beliefs may not necessarily be true. However, through constant thinking and repetition in your internal conversations, you have come to believe they are in fact true.

For example, my culture has a lot of beliefs that are passed from generation to generation, such as if you drink something cold you will get a sore throat, if you mix watermelon and milk you get a stomach ache, or if you don't wear a jacket you will get a cold, to name a few. These beliefs are not necessarily true but if I believe them to be true then it will limit me from doing and experiencing certain things in my life. These beliefs can become my own reality. The mind is constantly thinking negatively in terms of no, not, don't, and can't and most of the time, those negative words are false truths. They become true through the self-fulfilling prophecy and our believed internal beliefs. If you don't think you can do something, chances are you are not going to be able to do it or if you think you can't be good at something, then you will not be good at it.

Words have a unique meaning to each one of us, and therefore are very powerful. If we don't use the right words when communicating with ourselves, it could be self-destructing as they will become a part of our belief system. Carl Alasko Ph.D mentions that "Most of your self-esteem is what you make up about yourself and believe to be true." This is another reason why thought replacement or replacing your thoughts with positive thinking patterns is so important. You have the ability and can decide what you think about. Use positive affirmations to speak to yourself about who you are, what you want and who you want to be. With time and repetition, your subconscious mind will replace the old negative beliefs with new strong and powerful beliefs.

An affirmation is a powerful, positive statement that we repeat to ourselves. It encourages us, motivates us, inspires us, and even gives us that little push when we need it the most. Affirmations help us persevere and push us to continue to move forward when we fail. To use affirmations the right way, use powerful words like I am, I do, and I can. Add these words to your vocabulary and your daily self-talk. At first, some affirmations may not seem to be true to you, but with constant repetition, your subconscious mind will start to believe them and eventually, these affirmations will become your reality.

*See appendix for information on how to write your own affirmations, for a list of powerful words, and to see sample affirmations.

"Be careful how you talk to yourself
because you are listening."
Lisa M. Hayes

Exercise #3

Purpose: to communicate effectively with yourself and others. Listen carefully and provide correct feedback.

As we have learned, the process of effective communication can be quite challenging, that is, because we are not used to doing it the right way. With practice and repetition, you can learn to develop new habits and change the way you communicate with others and with yourself so that you can improve the overall well-being of your life.

For this exercise, be aware of how you are communicating and how others are communicating with you. Teach yourself how to listen and to always provide feedback to make sure the information you de-coded is the correct information.

While communicating effectively there is no such thing as a single word answer such as 'yes', 'no' or 'okay'. Follow your 'yes', 'no', or 'okay' answer with a statement about the conversation. For example, 'do you want to go to dinner?' don't just simply answer 'yes' or 'no'... answer with a complete sentence. 'Yes, I want to go to dinner.'

Also, pay attention to how you are speaking to your own self and replace negative self-talk with positive affirmations about yourself. For example, when you look at yourself in the mirror, instead of allowing your negative talk to take control of your mind with all the negative things you don't like about yourself, say an affirmation about yourself. If you look at yourself in the mirror and your self-talk says, 'I am getting old', recognize that negative thinking pattern and replace it with a positive affirmation such as 'I feel great at my age'.

Step #4

To Becoming
The Best Version of Yourself

STRESS

Stress

"The greatest weapon against stress
is our ability to choose
one thought over another."
William James

I am sure that at one point or another, you have heard or used the word stress to represent, illustrate, or try to explain how you are feeling. However, for most of us, it is difficult to say with precision what stress really is. Stress is a relative word as most people experience it in a different way or, to a different degree and level. One thing we know for sure is that stress is a normal part of our lives and it can be caused by the environment, our body, and our thoughts and thinking patterns.

Stress is our body's natural response to any change that requires adjustment or a response. In fact, it is part of life and fundamental to our survival. The body's natural response is actually a self-defense mechanism against danger and predators. To illustrate this idea more, let's use our imagination for a bit. Imagine you come across an animal or a bug that you fear. At the presence and, your mind's recognition of a fear or danger, the body naturally begins to flow with hormones that prepare the systems to confront or evade the threat. This amazing response is what is known as the fight or flight mechanism. Before we dig deeper into stress, lets first take a look at what the fight and flight response is.

Fight and Flight Response

When we are faced with a threatening, challenging, or terrifying situation (either mentally or physically), our bodies respond to these stressors by automatically triggering a 'fight or flight' response. As soon as stress is perceived, the sympathetic nervous system releases large quantities of hormones including epinephrine, norepinephrine, and cortisol. These chemicals cause a physical reaction as our bodies take over and rise to the occasion to fight the stressor. A variety of external and internal responses such as increased blood pressure, sweating, heightened muscle preparedness and alertness can accompany this chemical process. At the perception of a threat, an adrenaline spike causes your heart rate to speed-up—which increases oxygen flow, and your hearing is heightened while your perception of pain drops. All of these reactions are designed to improve a person's ability to quickly prepare to address the potential threat or dangerous situation at hand.

Although the 'fight and flight' response is designed to assess and respond to threats, it's important to note that it's not always accurate – and sometimes it may be activated by non-existent threats such as phobias. It can be triggered equally by real or imagined threats. The physical and psychological aspects of 'fight or flight' can absolutely exist and occur in an individual who perceives a threat that isn't real.

In addition to the fight or flight response, the human body may also respond to a threat or dangerous situation with what's referred to as the 'freeze' response.

Freeze Response

Although mostly everyone is familiar with the 'fight and flight' response, fewer people are aware of the 'freeze' response.

Just like 'fight and flight', the 'freeze' response is an involuntary and automatic response where the body decides that the best way of dealing with the threat is to shut down. The nervous system floods the bloodstream with stress hormones, just like the 'fight or flight'. The difference is that in the 'freeze' response, rather than prepare the body to fight or flee the scene of the threat, the nervous system decides that the best and safest response is to freeze, shutting down body systems in an attempt to be still and silent until the threat passes. The sympathetic and parasympathetic branches of our autonomic nervous system take control of the body in an effort to counterbalance the physical effects of the stress hormones flowing through the body. This causes the body to 'freeze', slowing down our heart rate and our breathing, which often feels like you can't breathe. The body might also feel cold and numb as pain-killing hormones are released into our system to reduce the physical and emotional responses. This experience can feel as if you are trapped within your own body.

The feeling of being paralyzed or 'frozen' is often associated with traumatic experiences where the physical impact of the stress hormones are magnified therefore causing extreme negative emotions like shock, panic, anxiety and terror. Unable to protect ourselves, the experience becomes too much and the brain shuts down, allowing a complete disconnection from the experience—which can alter the perception of reality. A great example of how the freezing response can be triggered in everyday events is the feeling that many people experience in stressful situations such as interviews, exams, social environment or conflict. A relatively normal amount of stress suddenly spirals out of control, and before you know it your mind goes blank. Everything stays shut down until the threat goes away—it is only then that we start to think clearly again and realize all the possible things we could have said or done in that moment.

In all, keep in mind that both the 'fight or flight' and 'freeze' responses are the body's way of keeping you safe, and therefore they are normal. These responses are automatic and are not conscious, therefore cannot be controlled. That is why it is important to constantly be aware of our stress levels around us so we can be more relaxed, more in control of our body, and have more clarity of thinking. According to Jami Deloe, ways to decrease the frequency in which the body goes into the 'freeze' response are grounding techniques, seeking help from a therapist and doing relaxation techniques which are going to be talked about in the following chapter.

Fear

As mentioned in step #2 to Becoming the Best Version of Yourself, we are creatures of habit and learn through repetition. Fears are unpleasant feelings and emotions induced by constant thinking and repetition; by an internal belief that someone or something is danger-ous and therefore likely to cause pain, or a threat. The amygdala is a part of the limbic system within the brain, and is responsible for emotions, survival instincts, and memory. It regulates our emotional responses and helps to store memories of events and emotions so that an individual may be able to recognize similar events in the future. The amygdala has priority over the neocortex (our thinking brain) and acts twice as fast as the frontal lobes (conscious rational decisions) to protect us.

For example, when you are stung by a bee, the amygdala helps process that event and therefore increases the fear or alertness around bees and it prepares the body to 'fight or flee'.

Back to Stress

Now that you have a better understanding about how stress triggers the 'fight, flight' and 'freeze' response caused by dangerous situations or fears, let's continue learning about stress.

It is hard to believe that even though the word stress is ingrained in our minds and is part of our everyday vocabulary, the term barely originated in the 1930's. Although, as mentioned by The American Institute of Stress, people commonly refer to stress as physical, mental, and emotional strain or tension. I want to introduce you to the definition given by the father of stress, Hans Selye.

Selye's definition of the term stress can be complex and difficult to understand as he defined stress as 'the non-specific response of the body to a demand for change'. Change, as we have been learning throughout this book, can be difficult in nature because it requires us to do something else. "To make or become different" is the definition of change in the dictionary. What Selye was referring to is to the fact that when there is change or a perceived change in the environment—our life, our thinking patterns or anything that we do—it will result in a response of our body caused by the change, therefore feeling stressed. For example, if you have plans to go to dinner on a given day, let's say at 7pm and you find out the day of the event that the dinner was changed to 6pm, the 'change' of time leads the body to feel stressed, as more than likely you had already planned your day around the fact that dinner was at 7pm. What Selye referred to as 'non-specific response of the body' means that the body is going to respond in a non-specific way; who knows how the body is going to respond, but it is going to respond. Common examples of how the body responds are:

- Blushing,
- Frowning,
- Sweaty hands,
- Shaking of the body,
- Twitches,
- Rapid movement of the legs, and
- Uncontrollable laugh to name a few.

General Adaptation Syndrome

For many years, it was believed that sickness was caused by specific and different pathogens. However, during Selye's numerous and extensive research with animals, he observed that physiological changes occurred in animals after being exposed to stressful events. The conclusion of the research proved that these changes or stressful events were not an isolated cause, but rather the typical response to stress. It was then that Selye developed the General Adaptation Syndrome stages which are a great tool to help us manage and better understand stress.

The 'fight and flight' as well as the 'freeze' response mentioned above occur during the first stage, also known as the alarm reaction stage—which refers to the initial symptoms the body experiences when it is under stress. During the second phase, known as the resistance stage, the body begins to repair itself by releasing cortisol which in turn help the body's heart rate and blood pressure to go back to normal. Even if the body is starting to repair itself, some stressful situations may stay present for a long period of time and if the stress is not controlled, the body will remain in high alert and eventually adapt and learn how to live with a high level of stress. A high stress level will continue to release hormones and the body's blood pressure will remain elevated. Even if you think you are managing stress well, your body will continue to react with physical changes. Signs of the resistance stage include frustration, poor concentration and irritability which can lead people to the third stage; the exhaustion stage. This third stage is the result of chronic or prolonged stress which can lead to draining your physical, emotional, and mental resources to continue to fight stress. During this stage, you may look at your life or situation as hopeless along with the feeling of wanting to give up. Signs of the exhaustion stage include burnout, fatigue, decreased tolerance, anxiety, and depression.

How to Manage Stress

When managing stress, it is of extreme importance to pay close attention to another term coined by Selye—the 'stressors.' Selye referred to the causes of stress as stressors, which are the reasons or the stimuli that cause stress. Reasons why a person might feel stressed can be anything your mind associates as being stressful including things like:

- Noise,
- Traffic,
- A first date,
- Doing dirty laundry,
- Washing dishes, to name a few.

Stressors are the things or events that lead us to feel stressed. To better explain this concept, let's use the example of rollercoasters.

Some people choose to sit in the front and feel excited, eyes open, screaming out of joy and usually cannot wait until the ride is over to ride it again. Others sit in the back, clenching their teeth, eyes closed, sweating and screaming out of fear. This example is used as an analogy to explain how stressors are different to each person, what distinguishes some people versus other people's perception of stress is the sense of control they had during the event. No person had more or less control during the rollercoaster experience, however their perspectives and expectations were different— which takes us back to the self-fulfilling prophecy; whatever you believe in, you are right.

The feeling of having little control or no control at all has been scientifically proven to be stressful, that is the reason and the importance of controlling the stressors. Stress is a part of our daily lives and in a way uncontrollable, as it may come to our awareness in numerous ways. Controlling the things that lead us to be stressed is the best way to relieving tension and stress. For example, if having dirty laundry stresses you, do laundry more consistently. Eliminating the stressor, in this case the accumulation of dirty clothes, will relieve you of the possible stress that comes from having dirty clothes.

According to Stanford University Medical School's research, an overwhelming 95% of illness and disease is attributed to stress. Scientifically, the most common causes for stress are:

- Relationships,
- The death of a loved one,
- Divorce,
- Loss of a job,
- Financial obligations,
- Chronic injury or illness,

- Emotional problems, and
- Traumatic events.

Meanwhile, while we might not be fully able to control stress, there are certain things we can do to maintain good mental health. The Mayo Clinic, a nonprofit organization committed to clinical practice, education and research, names numerous ways that can help with relieving stress. To relieve stress, you can:

- Exercise more,
- Eat healthier foods,
- Avoid unhealthy habits,
- Connect with others and nature,
- Get enough sleep,
- Keep a journal,
- Do meditation, yoga or relaxation techniques,
- Laugh more, and
- Seeking counseling.

*See appendix to take the Perceived Stress Scale and get an idea of what your stress levels are.

Magnifying Glass Analogy

I often use the magnifying glass analogy to exemplify how we see what we want to see and magnify what we want to magnify. The idea is to provide an example of something we can do when we have unwanted thoughts or thinking patterns that are leading us to feel stressed. It's just an analogy, but I have helped a lot of people understand this concept using this example.

Simply explained, a magnifying glass is a lens that produces an enlarged image. If you think about it, most of our issues, problems, or stress is something that we are consciously thinking about, meaning we have it in our conscious mind and make the decision to continuously think about it. In a way, we are choosing to magnify whatever information or situation we are dealing with; therefore, enlarging the image of that situation in our mind and making it more vivid or more real in our mind.

If you have ever looked through a magnifying glass, only one side of the lens magnifies the object. The opposite side actually makes the image smaller, as is the case for binoculars. If you turn them around, the image goes far, far away. Think of this as more than an analogy. Use it and apply this ideology in your daily life and push away the negativity, the thoughts and thinking patterns that are causing you to feel stressed. If the situation requires you to physically do something about it, take action to resolve the issues so that you are not magnifying the image, or the stress.

Keep in mind that from a mental perspective, energy, focus, and attention are three words that are closely related and regardless of the order you give to the words, one word leads to the next. For example, if you are constantly thinking or focusing on a problem, your energy, focus and attention are going towards that problem. The magnifying glass analogy, when applied in our lives, is meant to allow you to look at your problems or stress from a different lens and minimize them; always keeping in mind that you are in control of what you choose to think about.

Amor Fati

For many people, the past can be very stressful. We tend to overthink situations or problems from the past, constantly deciding to continue to think about those events and stressors over and over. Almost as if we couldn't free ourselves from the past. To steal a quote from Ben Courson, a lead pastor in Jacksonville, Oregon, "Your history does not define your destiny."

Stoicism is a school of Hellenistic philosophy born in Athens in the early third century. Amor fati which translated from Latin means love of fate is at the core of the Stoic philosophy and considered by many the formula for human greatness. Stoicism is an attitude designed to make us better. Its principle makes us more resilient, happier, more virtuous, and wiser. The Stoic mindset is about making the best of anything that happens in your life, good and bad, and embrace it. Not only to be okay with your past, but to love it and be better because of it. In a way, you wouldn't be where you are if it wasn't for your past. Even better yet, you wouldn't be *who you are* if not for your past making you better. Robert Greene, author of 48 Laws of Power, puts it like this "Accept the fact that all events occur for a reason, and that is within your capacity to see this reason as positive." That is not to say that good will always outweigh the bad, but as we know from Chevreul's pendulum, it is going to highly influence our body, so use anything bad in your life or your past, as a benefit because you are now better because of it. If you can believe that it happened because it was meant to happen, and you make the best of it, you can feel great about it even if it was difficult and painful. Amor fati is about embracing and loving what happens in life because that is what you decide to do.

Many people have hurt me or wronged me in one way or another and I can choose to look at them with despise or anger or choose to take the positives that I can take from the situation. I know that because of that person and the event, I am better than I was before. Those things are my choice, and my personal decision. One way I deal with situations like this is by knowing and understanding that I can only control myself and how I think, I am not responsible for others or the way they think and act. This allows me to live in peace knowing that I am living truthful to my morals, standards and values.

Ben Courson puts it best by using the analogy of playing music in a piano and says, "Even the black notes play music."

Forgiveness

Have you ever heard the phrase "We are our worst enemies?" A lot of us live our life haunted by our past or troubled by the mistakes we have made, and we allow those situations or circumstances to affect our present and our future. By allowing, and choosing to dwell on these traumas, we literally destroy ourselves internally. We become our worst enemy by the way we think and therefore live our lives filled with tension and stress from our past.

Inside of our subconscious mind we have stored all the memories from our past, both good and bad, as well as feelings, emotions, and sensations. When someone has hurt us, or we have hurt others and don't resolve or heal the situation, these memories affect and influence our individual well-being with feelings of hate, shame, guilt, anger, embarrassment, pain, and disappointment. I personally know these feelings well because of a traumatic event that happened to me as a kid. The experience changed my life forever, and the feelings and emotions led me to tears every time I thought about it; not to mention that for 8 years, I didn't talk about it with anyone. I thought it would be impossible to forgive and to forget. And although I have not forgotten the situation, I have learned to forgive and to be okay. I can now talk about it without feeling hatred and shame—and no longer cry about it. I have forgiven myself and forgiven the person that at thirteen years of age, tainted my life. Today, I understand the relationship between the mind and the body, I can see how for 8 years, by not telling anyone, I was affecting my growth and damaging my own life. Not forgiving was destructive to my present, and worse yet, manipulating my future.

Aside from cultural beliefs, religious inclination, or scientific explanations, to forgive can be extremely beneficial to your health and to your well-being. To forgive means, to stop feeling anger or resentment toward someone for an offense, mistake, or flaw. It does not mean that what others did is no longer wrong, it means that you find it in your heart to free yourself—to let go and move on. Forgiving yourself and others is a healthy practice that can help you reduce tension and stress from the past. When you become right with others, you also become right with yourself. Through Amor fati, we learned that we can decide to embrace everything that has happened to us and come to love and accept what happened because it made us better.

There are multiple ways and processes in which individuals can come to understand and accept forgiveness as a path to better relationships and a better life.

Personally, a technique that I have used and that I have had a lot of success with when dealing with forgiveness, is a Hawaiian technique called Ho'oponopono. It is an incredible process of forgiveness to heal yourself, other people, and the world around you. The best part about this technique is that you can do it in your own mind, as the power of this ancient technique is in the feelings and willingness to forgive and to love.

*See appendix for information on how to practice the Ho'oponopono process.

"It's not stress that kills us,
it is our reaction to it."
Hans Selye

Exercise # 4

Purpose: to eliminate stressors by finding the stressors in your life, creating a plan, and relieving yourself from stress.

Stress is a powerful word. This six-letter word has the power to control every aspect of our being and our life. That is, if we allow it. What I mean by saying, if we allow it, is that although we might not be able to control stress, we are in a lot more control than we think we are. Each and every one of us is responsible for the things we think about. All of our lives are filled with stressful situations, that we rarely ever take the time to assess the best possible way to eliminate the stress. We allow our mind to consume itself by what we choose to think about. This exercise is an action-based exercise.

Through awareness, you can pay attention in your own life and identify the very same things that are leading you to feel stressed. Once you have identified the stressor, you are to create a plan to eliminate the source of stress by taking action. This is a challenging exercise because it is going to push you past your comfort zone, however, it is important to understand that if it is causing you stress, it probably shouldn't be a part of your life. Be in control of your-self, and be brave enough to confront the situation, to speak to that person, to take care of yourself, or to develop a plan. Ultimately, the only way you are going to eliminate stress from your life is by doing something about it.

Remember, it is not about why you are stressed, it is about what you are going to do about it. If the stress is constantly in your mind and present in your life, the stress will be controlling you. You are in charge. Control the stressors, and the stress in your life will diminish.

What is stressing you?

_____

What is the stressor?

_____

How can you eliminate it?

_____

What are you going to do?

_____

Step #5

To Becoming
The Best Version of Yourself

RELAXATION

Relaxation

"Take a deep breath
inhale peace,
exhale happiness."
A.D. Posey

Have you been on a vacation and you came home more tired, more stressed and more overwhelmed than before you left? Has anyone ever asked you what you are doing, and you respond that you are 'relaxing'? Have you ever tried to 'relax' and you just can't do it? I can think of numerous times where these situations have happened in my life and I know the unpleasant feeling of trying to slow down when I have so many things on mind but cannot do it.

Through the years I have learned to truly relax and allow my mind to be free of any tension and anxiety. I used to live my life with such an enormous amount of information in my head that I found it difficult to rest or to sleep as my brain was always running at full speed and it was very difficult to slow it down. Now, I live with an internal peace and in control of my thoughts and thinking patterns, and I am able to relax and enjoy the wonders that life has to offer. I am making the most of each and every day, and living to the max.

There are three things we can all control if we work on them— what you decide to think about, the images you see in your head (visualization), and the actions you take (behavior). I too used to think I was constantly relaxing throughout the day, but it wasn't until I truly learned to fade away negativity and control the images in my brain that I truly knew what it was like to live a relaxing life.

Our minds are filled with these things, that everyone in the world experiences:

- Tension,
- Stress,
- Problems,
- Fears,
- Roadblocks, and
- Limitations.

These six factors make it difficult for us to relax. Add other information you may have on your mind such as to-do lists, work, relationships, our children etc. and you will realize our minds are constantly overwhelmed with large amounts of information. It is very difficult, almost impossible, to relax when the mind is busy or preoccupied with information. In fact, the mind is not designed to have more than one thought or thinking pattern at the same time. It is not possible to have multiple feelings, emotions, and sensations at the same time. You cannot be sad and be happy at the same time or be hot and cold at the same time. Our brain is so perfectly designed that it only allows us to deal with one feeling, one emotion, or one sensation at the time.

Let's do a quick exercise to prove this point. While sitting, raise your right foot off the floor and start turning, or making circles with your ankle to the right (clockwise). As you are doing this, with your right index finger draw a number 6 in the air. What happens? Your foot will turn to the left (counterclockwise) and you cannot control it. Two different indications are being given to you, in other words, two multiple thinking patterns at the same time. To spin your foot clockwise, and do a number six in the air, which is counterclockwise, so your brain combines both thinking patterns and joins them into one.

If you have wondered why you are getting more tired, stressed, or overwhelmed while 'relaxing' at home, during a vacation, or anywhere you may be, the answer is because your mind is filled or overloaded with information. In this step you are going to learn how to breath correctly, how to clear your mind, truly relax, and visualize correctly so you can experience life in a more relaxing and joyful way.

Clarity of Thinking

'Just clear your mind', 'don't think about it', and 'let it go' are all very common phrases used by people. I am sure at one point or another someone has told you one of these phrases, or you have told someone something similar. However, some things are easier said than done. The ability to think clearly can be a very difficult process to accomplish if we don't know how to do it. The white bear theory is a great way to exemplify this concept.

The white bear theory refers to the psychological process whereby deliberately attempting to suppress certain thoughts makes them more likely to surface. For example, if I said to you, don't think of a blue horse, now a blue horse has been brought to your attention, to your awareness, and your mind is going to choose to think or imagine a blue horse. In order for you to not think about a certain thing, first, you have to think of that very same thing and then make a decision to replace your thoughts and thinking patterns so that you can start thinking of something else. If you are still thinking about the blue horse, it is because you are making a decision to think about a blue horse. If you want to stop thinking about the blue horse, understand that first, you are going to think about the blue horse because it has been brought to awareness; then, consciously override the blue horse with a new thinking pattern. Remember, you get to think about whatever it is you want to think about. You are one hundred percent in control of your thinking. No one can think for you or tell you what to think about. You always have the option and final decision to think about whatever it is that you want to think about.

To have clarity of thinking refers to one's ability to gather and differentiate all incoming information into a clear definition so that we can position the mind with resolve. In other words, if we clearly understand the information coming in, we can choose whether or not we want to continue thinking about that or, we can decide to think about something else. We have the ability to focus on what really matters.

Relaxation or being in a relaxed state of mind is the foundational key to being able to think clearly. However, there are certain things we can all do to help ourselves get to a place where we are in control of the mind instead of the mind being in control of us. This is paramount because when we allow the mind to take control, we are short-tempered, feel overwhelmed, frustrated, angry, and completely out of control.

Thinking clearly can help us make better decisions, do more meaningful work, become more trusting, have better relationships and can improve the overall well-being of our life.

To develop better clarity of thinking try the following:

- Generate space: Clear the clutter from your life and reset back to a place that is comfortable for you to get things done. No one can work effectively with a mess or live thoughtfully in chaos.

- Do one thing at a time: Be where you need to be when you need to be there. If you are writing, write. If you are eating, eat. We often don't enjoy our life because we are constantly multi-tasking and we are neither accomplishing one thing or another. Immerse yourself in the task at hand.

- Identify what matters: Make a list of your to-dos' and prioritize what is really important and what needs to get done as soon as possible. Many of the things on your mind can wait.

- Eliminate distractions: Research shows that it can take up 15 minutes or more to recover from distractions. Turn off your beeps and dings from your phone, messages on the computer, or any distraction that could take your focus away from the task at hand.

- Write to get clear: Writing a few minutes a day, on your phone or a piece of paper can help your mind be more at ease because you know the information is written down so you can get back to it at a later time.

- Experiment: You don't know what you don't know, so try to learn new things. Sometimes small changes like a new routine, new food, or new habit in our life can give us more clarity and peace of mind. Quit watching TV, cut down on sugar, wake up earlier, or minimize salt intake but experiment with something new.

Clarity of mind allows us to think more clearly because there is less confusion and doubt in our mind. But it requires discipline, commitment, and small changes in the way we do things. I highly encourage you to take a deeper look into your life and adjust the things in your life that may be clouding your thinking. Simplicity comes with amazing benefits and at the top of the list is the ability to think more clearly. If you want more clarity of thinking, focus on what truly matters and get rid of everything that doesn't.

Relaxation

Just for fun I googled the word relax, and as of the writing of this book, I got an astonishing 1,630,000,000 hits. Without even looking at results themselves, this number tells me that people are desperate to find ways to unwind. It happens to all of us. We look down the road, and see the summer is getting closer, and we are looking forward to relaxing. But somehow, it doesn't happen. It happens to people of all ages, races, ethnicities, and backgrounds. We all plan to relax, and it ends up not happening.

Our minds are influenced by our bodies and vice versa, our bodies are influenced by our minds. We all know that in order to be healthy, we need to eat well, exercise, and rest. So, we work at developing better eating habits and we work at exercising, but when it comes to resting, the vast majority of people feel bad or guilty about having down time. As we learned in the previous section, physiologically, stress triggers the sympathetic nervous system—the 'fight' and 'flight' response. What's more, is that scientific research shows that we get stressed about relaxing because we work hard in all areas of our life and it makes it difficult to just let go. We work so hard at relaxing that it becomes stressful to relax.

The daily demands of our life are intense and never ending. As mentioned by Diane Barth, L.C.S.W. "We have come to equate success with achievement, and achievement with happiness." Furthermore, research has shown that stress, anxiety and depression—which come on the heels of this kind of non-stop pressure to achieve—physically interfere with the body's relaxation mechanism. "And of course, focusing on relaxation as yet another high-pressure goal, is not going to cut it."

Although we are used to going hard 24 hours a day, 7 times a week, and 365 days a year, our bodies were not designed to do that. We need to give ourselves a break, have some down time or take a day off. Not doing so can be more counterproductive as our mind will be overwhelmed with information and our body will suffer the consequences. Relaxation is the state of being free from stress and anxiety, which means we must learn to relax, and slow down. We simply cannot go full speed all the time without the mind and body being affected.

Importance of Relaxation

According to Allan Schwartz LCSW, Ph.D. relaxation must be on the top of everyone's list of priorities. Relaxation reduces the wear and tear on the mind and body, and it is essential to living a healthy life-style. As we previously learned, relaxation is fundamental to having a clear mind and when we have a clear mind, we can make better decisions. Being in a relaxed state can be the difference between being and feeling in control or being erratic and all over the place.

Relaxation is essential to the mind and body connection and it allows us to have self-control. It helps us to redirect thoughts, feelings, and emotions to the things that truly matter. It helps us to be more efficient when we need it most. Relaxation slows things down and it is fundamental to enter a flow-state of mind, where you are in total control of whatever activity it is that you are doing.

Flow, also known as the zone, is the mental state of operation in which a person performing an activity is fully immersed in a feeling of energized focus, full involvement, and enjoyment in the process of the activity. Most people have experienced this amazing phenomenon and have felt what it is like to be in flow. As kids, you might remember when you were playing outside and you were totally one hundred percent invested in what you were doing. You were truly enjoying the moment, and time felt like it was speeding up. By the time you realized what time of day it was, you could hardly believe that so much time had passed by. I remember all these times I would be outside playing baseball early in the day and then I would hear my mom call me for dinner. How did time go so fast? I was in flow. Other people may experience flow at work, on trips, or even doing schoolwork. You get so immersed and involved in what you are doing that by the time you look at the clock, you can hardly understand how time went by so quickly. You were in flow.

Psychologist Mihali Csikszentmihalyi's famous investigations on optimal experience have revealed that what makes an experience genuinely satisfying is the state of consciousness called 'flow.' Optimal experience can only happen through truly enjoying what we are doing, and to enjoy what we are doing, you must be in a relaxed state of mind. Therefore, optimal experience is something we can make happen if we allow ourselves to relax and enjoy our life. As mentioned by Csikszentmihalyi, flow is complete focused motivation. It is a single-minded immersion and represents perhaps the ultimate experience in harnessing the emotions in the service of performing and learning. In flow, the emotions are not just contained and channeled, they are also positive, energized, and aligned with the task at hand.

Csikszentmihalyi identifies six essential factors when encompassing an experience of flow:

1. Intense and focused concentration on the present moment.
2. Merging of actions and awareness.
3. A loss of reflective self-consciousness.
4. A sense of personal control over the situation or activity.
5. A distortion of temporal existence, one's subjective experience of time is altered.
6. Experience of the activity as intrinsically rewarding.

The hallmark of flow is a feeling of spontaneous joy, even rapture, while performing a task. It is the goal of this book, that through practice and repetition of the 7 Steps to Becoming the Best Version of Yourself, you can get as close as you can to experiencing this amazing phenomenon as much and as consistently as possible.

What Happens When You Relax?

When you relax, blood flow increases in your body and it gives you more energy. It leads you to be calmer, to have a clear mentality, and be more in control—which in turn aids your positive thinking, concentration, memory, and decision-making process.

Relaxing consistently throughout the day decreases your heart rate and your breathing becomes slower and deeper. Blood pressure drops and stabilizes, and your muscles relax. Your digestive system and hormonal levels return to normal. It also allows your body to recuperate so that the body can begin to heal. Relaxing counteracts the stress chemicals that are released into the body when we are stressed.

Do What Relaxes You!

The ocean, the beach. The hot tub, a long hot shower. The woods, the lake. Sipping a cup of tea, people watching. Jogging, riding my bike. Doing a jig-saw puzzle. These are all examples of things that relax me. You may relate to a few of these, or you might not and that is totally fine. These are things that as I mentioned before, relax me. The idea is that you identify what activities or things that you do relax you so that you can practice them more consistently throughout the day.

When this topic is brought up in the conversations that I have with many of the athletes and people I work with, there is usually confusion as to certain activities they do, that they think are relaxing but turn out to be stressful. A common example I can give you is playing video games. A lot of people like playing video games and they consider video game playing a relaxing activity but then I ask them if playing video games upsets them or makes you angry when they lose? And the common answer is yes. So, if while playing video games, you are getting upset or angry, how is that relaxing?

Relaxing or getting to a relaxed state is different for everyone. Some people feel relaxed when taking deep breaths or doing breathing exercises, others by soaking on a warm bath or listening to soothing music. Whatever activity relaxes you, practice it more regularly so you can be in a relaxed state more consistently. Remember, relaxation or being relaxed is fundamental to have clarity of thinking.

Breathing

At 12 weeks during pregnancy, the left and right lobes of the lungs of a fetus start to grow and branch out small contractions that stimulate the chest muscles to develop. As early as 15 weeks of pregnancy, breathing movements can already be seen in the utero and from the minute we are born, within 10 seconds, we start to breathe fresh air. Breathing is usually a subconscious habit; we don't think about breathing, we simply just breathe. In fact, the average person breathes about 22,000 to 24,000 times per day. Think about it, when was the last time you actually spent time thinking about how you breathe?

Adults use the coordination of three muscle groups to breathe; the diaphragm, intercostal muscles or the muscles between each rib, and the abdominal muscles. When the diaphragm pulls down, air enters the lungs and when the diaphragm relaxes, air is naturally expelled. The intercostal muscles pull the lungs outwardly while the abdominal muscles help the diaphragm to pull down and fill the lungs with air. Babies on the other hand, will use their abdominal muscles more, as their intercostal muscles are not fully developed at the time of birth.

A healthy newborn child breathes anywhere from 30-60 times per minute and for up to six months newborns will only breathe through their nose. Newborns sleep on their backs and wrapped so that nothing interferes with the baby's nostrils. Any compromise to the baby's nose will block the baby's airways and will not allow oxygen to enter the body and carbon dioxide to leave the body. When babies breathe, their whole bodies fill up with air and you can clearly see how the stomach inflates and deflates as they breathe.

From the minute we were born, we all breathe and during the first months of life, as babies, will learn to breathe not only through our nose, but also through our mouth. As we continue to develop, somewhere along the lines most people will start to breathe more with the chest than with the belly. When it happens or why it happens is a question that has puzzled scientists and researchers for a long time. The fact of the matter is that at some point we have to pay attention to how we breathe, whether it is through our nose or mouth, and whether it is with our belly or our chest. Understanding and identifying how we breathe can be incredibly beneficial to our life and is also essential to relaxing more efficiently.

Proper Breathing

Before we talk about the proper way of breathing, let's take a look at how you breathe. For this exercise, clear your mind for a second and take a few deep breaths. Now, how did you breathe? Did you take a deep breath through your mouth, or your nose? If you took a breath with your nose, good job. If you took a breath with your mouth, it may be time to start being conscious of your breathing and work towards breathing through your nose more consistently.

Breathing through your nose is scientifically proven to be a more efficient way to breathe. As you breathe through your nose the incoming air travels through two narrow passages and the resistance to the intake of air slows things down, giving you a nice, slow, deep breathing pattern. As you inhale through your nose, the air is warmed and humidified while the fine hairs in the nasal passage filter any possible debris and clean out your nostrils. Nose breathing provides about 50% more resistance than mouth breathing—what is more, breathing through the mouth does not have a filter system to protect the rest of the respiratory system.

Breathing through your mouth has its benefits as well, as it allows us to get air into the lungs more quickly and increase oxygen intake. However, breathing through the mouth is a bad habit and should only be used in temporary situations like when you are panting to catch up your breath or when gasping for air. Other reasons why we might not breathe through the nose include nasal congestions, injuries to the nose, stress, and out of habit.

When I was a baby and for most of my childhood I dealt with sinusitis, or sinus infections which made it extremely difficult for me to breathe through my nose. As a result, I developed the bad habit of breathing through my mouth and like all habits, I had to re-learn and train myself to breathe through my nose again. In order to change a bad habit, we have to be consciously aware of what we are doing so that we can take action to change the old habit. By being conscious of my breathing I was able to go back to breathing through my nose. In the same manner, you too can be aware of how you breathe and work towards breathing through your nose as much as possible for optimal health. Mouth breathing should only act as a backup for when we need quick air.

Diaphragmic Breathing

During the nose and mouth breathing identification exercise, did you notice whether you were breathing with your chest or your belly? If you don't remember, let's try the exercise again, clear your mind for a few seconds, take a couple of deep breaths through your nose and pay attention to whether you are breathing with your chest, or your belly.

Diaphragmatic breathing as it is known, can often be misleading because all forms of breathing involve using the diaphragm. Belly breathing, abdominal breathing, or diaphragm breathing refers to breaths that move the belly whereas, thoracic breathing, or chest breathing refers to breaths that move the rib cage. Whether one way or the other is better or worse depends on the person and the intention of the practice. For relaxation purposes, I have found belly breathing to be more efficient and therefore encourage all people to breathe through the nose and with the belly as it pulls down on your lungs, creating negative pressure in the chest and resulting in air flowing to your lungs.

When you breathe properly with your belly, the process starts in the nose and then moves to the stomach and as your diaphragm contracts, your belly expands, and your lungs fill with air.

One of the most important benefits of breathing with your abdomen is the reduction of stress however other benefits include but are not limited to the fact that:

- It helps you relax.
- It lowers your heart rate.
- It helps lower your blood pressure.
- It helps you cope with symptoms of post-traumatic stress disorder (PTSD).
- It improves your core stability.
- It improves your body's ability to tolerate intense exercise.
- It lowers your chances of injuring or wearing out your muscles.
- It slows your rate of breathing so that it expends less energy.

In all, every system in the body relies on oxygen. From cognition to digestion, effective breathing can not only provide you with a greater sense of mental clarity, but also can help you sleep better, digest food more efficiently, improve your body's immune response, and reduce stress levels.

We all want to relax and take our mind and body to a peaceful place where we can just enjoy the present moment. However, the truth is most people in the world either don't breathe correctly, or don't know how to slow down their mind. Breathing and relaxation techniques are a great way to manage stress, to allow us to slow down, and to have clarity of thinking. Breathing and relaxation are both a skill that can be learned with practice and repetition. To master any art, we must practice consistently so I encourage you to try and practice the following breathing and relaxation techniques so that you can find yourself in more control of your mind, and therefore more relaxed.

Breathing and Relaxation Techniques

Research indicates that there is a correlation between the way you breathe and the way you think and feel. However, we rarely ever pay attention to how we breathe. The following are techniques that I practice and teach to all the people I work with. The techniques are to be practiced by breathing through your nose and your abdomen or belly.

To prepare for relaxation:

1. Find a quiet place free from distractions.
2. Lie on the floor or sit comfortably in a chair.
3. Loosen any tight clothing.
4. Rest your arms, hands, and legs. Do not cross your arms or legs.

*For more relaxation techniques such as autogenic training, meditation, and mindfulness go to the appendix.

Combat Tactical Breathing or 4 by 4

This time-honored stress reducing technique is endorsed by none other than the U.S. Navy SEALs. For SEALs, this technique is a way to stay calm and focused –and therefore alive—before, during, after intense combat. For all of us who are not military trained, it is an amazing simple technique to keep everyday stress in check.

1. Inhale for 4 seconds or a count of four.
2. Hold the air for 4 seconds or a count of four.
3. Exhale for 4 seconds or a count of four.
4. Hold your breath without air for 4 seconds or a count of four.

Repeat this process as many times as needed or until feeling calm and back in control of your thinking patterns. I find this technique incredible powerful because it distracts the mind from our problems or stress we have in our mind. As mentioned in a previous exercise, we cannot have multiple thinking patterns in our mind at the same time, so this technique focuses on counting the 4 seconds or the count of four.

4 by 4 Modified

Similar to the Combat Tactical Breathing technique, this is the technique I use most often with athletes or people who are in some type of competition. It differs from the previous technique because there is no hold after inhalations or exhalations. Simply inhale for 4 seconds or a count of four and without holding your breath, exhale for four seconds or a count of four.

1. Inhale for 4 seconds or a count of four.
2. Exhale for 4 seconds or a count of four.

3. Inhale for 4 seconds or a count of four.
4. Exhale for 4 seconds or a count of four.

Repeat this process as many times as needed or until feeling calm and back in control of your thinking patterns.

4-7-8 or Relaxing Breath

This breathing technique aims to reduce anxiety or help people get to sleep.

1. Exhale completely through your mouth making a whoosh sound.
2. Inhale through your nose to a count of 4.
3. Hold for a count of 7.
4. Exhale through your mouth making a whoosh sound to a count of 8.

Meditation and Mindfulness

The human mind wanders, there is no doubt about that. Although the focus goal of both meditation and mindfulness are different, both techniques can take you to a place of internal peace and tranquility. Meditation can be best explained as the awareness of 'no-thing' while mindfulness is the awareness of 'some-thing'.

Meditation is an intentional practice where you focus inwardly to increase calmness, emotional balance, and concentration. The idea is to go beyond the mind and experience our essential nature. Meditation focuses on bringing your attention to your breath, your inhalations and exhalations, and consciously guide your mind to a single point of focus—a mantra. Mindfulness in the other hand, is all about actively being aware of thoughts, movement, feelings, and behavior. Mindfulness focuses on the acceptance of the present moment rather than dwelling on the past or dreading about the future. Being mindful refers to the person's awareness of all existing surroundings. In mindfulness, there is no room for interpretation or judgement.

Personally, I encourage people to make relaxation a part of their lives first before venturing into practicing meditation and mindfulness. Most people don't know how to relax, so it is important to gain control of your mind first in order to then move on into more detailed and structured techniques. However, I wanted to make reference of meditation and mindfulness in case you are more advanced and want to venture into practicing these techniques.

*In the appendix section of this book, I have included different meditation and mindfulness techniques for you to practice.

"Sometimes
the most productive thing you can do
is relax."
Mark Black

Exercise #5

Purpose: to breathe correctly and relax consistently. Set daily time aside to relax and while relaxing, breathe through your nose and with the stomach.

Because breathing is something natural that we all do, we rarely ever take the time to make sure that we are breathing correctly through the nose. This exercise is about consistently being aware of how you are breathing so that you can breathe correctly. At the same time, it is about consistently relaxing throughout the day, every day.

Find time in your schedule to allow yourself to relax a minimum of three times per day, even if it is for just a few minutes. Allow your stress levels to go down by relaxing and focusing your mind into your breathing and therefore your body. Do what will help you to relax. There's an incredible number of ways to relax, and hundreds if not thousands of relaxation techniques. Find and practice the relaxations that work for you and begin experiencing what it is like to be in control of the mind.

If you experience some type of emotional discomfort or anxiety while performing relaxation, consider talking to a doctor or mental health professional. There is no shame in asking for help if you feel you are running into trouble.

* To receive a free relaxation PDF and audio, sign up at www.thechoicetobelieve.com

Step #6

To Becoming
The Best Version of Yourself

ATTITUDE

Attitude

"There are some people that would
rather die, than quit."
Unknown

Since you're reading a book about mental toughness and personal development, I don't think I have to tell you that the attitude in which a person approaches any life situation is going to greatly affect—or even determine—the outcome of that scenario. A good attitude is something that we are told to have since we are children, but we aren't necessarily taught how to achieve it. We are naturally drawn to people who have positive attitudes, and often individuals with a good attitude are more popular and successful. The pull is almost magnetic. We just want to be around people who bring light and enthusiasm to the things they do; even when we are not that way ourselves. So, is having a good attitude a personality trait you are naturally gifted with? Or is it a skill? In other words, is someone simply born a positive person, or is it a quality that is learned and practiced over time?

Attitude is a way of thinking or feeling and refers to emotions, beliefs, and behaviors towards a person, object, thing or event. While general disposition—how upbeat or grumpy a person is on a regular basis—can be a personality trait we are born with, our attitude is often influenced by our experiences and our upbringing. Attitudes can be enduring but they can also be changed. If you want to have the best chances for success in life, you must want to approach life with a better attitude. Having a good attitude like most things in life, is a skill that with work and practice can be learned and improved upon.

There's something really important to understand with regards to attitude. Success isn't only about being happy, positive and optimistic, and never having negative emotions. More importantly, it's about understanding that negative and positive feelings, emotions and sensations are all a part of life. Having a strong mentality is about being able to control your mind and about how quickly you can return to your normal self when things don't go your way—instead of letting a poor attitude derail you from being the best version of yourself. Ultimately, your attitude reflects your leadership—towards others, but most importantly, to yourself.

When it comes to learning any aspect of mental toughness or mental training, I like to use examples and inspirational stories to make concepts more relatable. And when it comes to finding role models to exemplify attitude and leadership, I have a few favorites.

Kobe

Aside from your personal preference, there is no argument that Kobe Bryant was born with a level of athletic talent that was out if this world. His natural skills on the basketball court could have been enough to make almost anyone successful, but the thing that set him apart and made him an all-time great was his attitude. The way he approached every aspect of his sport with commitment and tenacity. Kobe Bryant was literally the definition of what it looked like to do whatever it takes. This was brought to my attention in 2003 when I was playing college baseball. My coach at the University of San Diego, Rich Hill, used Kobe Bryant's rock-solid dedication to help me understand the difference between the words 'can't' and 'want'. Through the years, I've learned to apply this mentality of doing whatever it takes (which I call the Kobe Mentality) to situations involving a number of different scenarios and it is a concept I often talk to my clients about.

Here's what happened. Early in the season, I hurt my index finger in my throwing hand. After several doctor appointments, I was told I had a torn ligament, and that even though the ligament was damaged, it couldn't get any worse. The doctor said that I could still play if I could handle the pain. Shortly after, I met with my coach to talk about the diagnosis and I said to him that I couldn't play because I was hurt. My coach looked at me straight in the eyes and said, "I already talked to the doctor, so I know the situation. My question to you is, you can't play? or you won't play?" Then, he proceeded… "Kobe Bryant plays no matter what-- because that is who he is, he does whatever it takes." I was speechless for a minute, but the comment hit me where it hurts the most, in my ego. My coach knew that the ligament was torn, and it couldn't get any worse, and he challenged me and my way of thinking. Was I willing to do whatever it took?

I had already given up the idea of playing because my finger was hurt, and I was choosing not to play because of it. Being reminded of the way that Kobe Bryant would handle a similar situation hit my ego in a big way, but it changed me; Kobe's mentality was an example of someone who had an amazing attitude. So, I changed my mindset and decided to play. Making that decision boosted my self-esteem and made me realize that I had the power to have a great attitude. It was going to be painful and challenging, but I could do it. If Kobe could do it, so could I. My coach was right. Kobe's mental strength allowed him to play with a sore and hurt body; he even played with broken fingers and a broken nose. It would take more than an injury to get Kobe off the court. His entire career, Kobe was known for incredible work ethic and desire to improve. He practiced the same shot over and over again for hours. Kobe gave everything he had until he didn't have anything left to give, and then some. He did whatever it took.

I played most of the 2003 season with a half cast and a torn ligament—and it wasn't always pretty! That year, I was close to breaking the NCAA record for errors. The season was full of ups and downs, and it was really painful at times. But the valuable lesson I learned that day was one that I took with me the rest of my career and to this day, I continue to apply in my everyday life. There is a huge difference between the words 'can't' and 'won't'. There are times when we fixate our minds on the belief that we can't do something only because we are not willing to go through pain and adversity. There are times we don't do whatever it takes to succeed.

The Kobe Mentality is applicable to so many things – from schooling and career related challenges, to sports injuries and surgeries. It's extremely helpful when you are in physical pain and you think you can't to do something because it will hurt. Following the example set by this great athlete, you can make the decision that you are willing to do whatever it takes. And a huge element of this mentality is the ability to separate and clearly identify what you can't do versus what you won't do. Push through the doubts and question the idea that you 'can't' do the task in front of you. With the right attitude, you can do anything you want, which in turn, will give you the best chance to be successful. Do whatever it takes.

U.S. Navy SEAL Mentality

Ever since I learned about the U.S. Navy SEAL Special Forces, I have been fascinated with their training, determination, and commitment. Their unique resilience and grit distinctively make them some of the most mentally strong people in the world. Although we cannot ignore the accomplishment of other special forces, the Navy SEALs are considered to be the best special operation forces on our planet. What makes them so extraordinary? Their uniquely strong mentality: It takes death to break a Navy SEAL.

Simply put, Navy SEALs will lay their lives on the line to get the job done. There are so many reasons that the Navy SEALs are a stellar example of what it looks like to have a good attitude – but there is one thing that comes to the forefront of my mind. For a SEAL, failure is not even an option. There are no valid excuses. It is the mentality and the attitude of 'you have to kill me in order for me to not finish my mission.' If you think about it, we all have missions in our lives. We all have responsibilities, tasks, and goals and although they are not necessary war related—and we might not lose our lives over the outcome—we all go through different wars in our minds every day. We all have things to accomplish, goals to achieve, or things we want to change in our life to become the best version of ourselves. For most people, in most cases, attitude changes as life circumstances change and sometimes our attitude is great, but some other times it is garbage.

But here's the most important concept to grasp about the idea of attitude as it relates to the Navy SEALs: How you see yourself in the specific environment that you are in can dictate how you deal with it in your mind. If failure is not an option, your attitude will push you forward.

Research shows that high failure rate is not because of the lack of skills or knowledge, but because of the attitude people have. The SEAL's mentality is to do whatever it takes, no matter the circumstance or the situation, and without the option of failure. With this mentality, you just show up, you do what you have to do, and you move forward because you understand that your attitude influences your behavior and a good attitude gets you better results.

Next time you are faced with a challenging situation, remember that your attitude can change the way you think, act, and feel. Be aware and in control of your mind to be able to check where your attitude is in that moment. If it is not in the right place, do what you have to do to change it and put yourself in the best possible scenario to succeed. Then, ask yourself if you are willing to do whatever it takes to improve yourself. Are you willing to put yourself through hell for the well-being of your family? Or your kids? Do you have the attitude and mentality of doing whatever it fu#%$@! takes to turn yourself or your life around? In today's world we are accustomed to the fact that things in life come easy—but they don't, and your attitude will either make you or break you. The Navy SEAL attitude leaves no room for excuses, you do whatever it takes as if your life depended on it; If you have to drive 100 miles to get to work, or if you have to wake up at 4am each day, you do it because failing is not an option. The right attitude will bring constructive changes to your life, make you happier, and will make you more successful. Do what you have to do as if your life depended on it, failure is not an option.

Just Do It Mentality

Can you imagine what it would be like to be an advertising executive, responsible for a slogan that has inspired and challenged entire generations of athletes and consumers? I think it is an incredible way to impact the world through creativity.

Growing up, I was afraid of a lot of things. No one really knew it, because I didn't share it with anyone, but I struggled a lot with fears inside my own mind. When I was about 10 years old, I started to become aware of the Nike brand and I began to see the signature Nike swoosh everywhere. I distinctly remember the first time I came across Nike's slogan: "Just Do It." It seemed so simple, but for a young kid fighting fears inside his mind, it basically jumped off the billboard and into my mind. The Nike slogan became a personal challenge that changed my life. Just Do It. I felt like the message was personally for me and I adopted it as a new mentality to overcome fears and move myself towards my goals.

I remember consistently repeating the words 'Just Do It' to myself through the most challenging moments in my childhood. I remember how good I felt when I overcame those challenging moments and experienced internal satisfaction and victory. I believe that most of us have fears and are frequently allowing ourselves to be limited by those thinking patterns. Fears are mental blockages that can prevent us from living and achieving the life we want. Some people fear the unknown of the future and/or fear failing, which leads them to not even try. When I have felt fear rising up within me, I have been able to confront that fear with the statement 'Just Do It'. Almost everyone in the world has some kind of a fear, some are minor or unimportant fears, but others can lead to anxiety and interfere with our normal life. I know I have fears and up to this day, I challenge myself to push through those fears. I know and understand that fears start in my mind and that I have the power to either magnify that fear by continuously think about it, or the power to replace my thinking patterns and overcome it. I choose to make the decision in my mind, to think and repeat to myself that I can do it. It is that simple, I just do it.

To clarify, I am not saying that overcoming fears is simple or easy. The most important factor to understand is that the actual initial decision in my mind—the one where I stop the fear in its tracks by confronting it—is a very simple decision to make. I tell myself to 'Just Do It'. It is just a thought being replaced with a new thinking pattern. You can go from thinking and believing you can't do it, or you won't do it, to knowing that you are doing it. The basics of this mentality have helped me and many of my clients to cope with the affairs of daily life. Be mindful that your attitude towards life and challenges has a profound impact on your success; change your attitude and you will change your life. It's one of the most powerful things you can do. Just do it!

Now that we have gone over a few examples of how attitude can directly affect your success in life, I would like to touch on a couple of other over-arching topics that will give you a better understanding of attitude. Everything you have learned in this book (if actively practiced) can be applied towards cultivating a positive, strong, and powerful good attitude.

Toxicity

I mentioned earlier that having a good attitude is not all about being externally happy and positive all the time. I want to expand on that a little more, because it is really important. Every human being has a mindset that influences how they view the world around them. Some do it in a healthy way, while others are constantly creating obstacles in their mind that get in the way of happiness and success. Toxicity comes into our lives through external circumstances or by how we think, but most importantly, it comes into our lives because we allow it. We surround ourselves with toxic people, get involved in toxic relationships, and constantly compare ourselves to others. We pretend to live perfect lives and sabotage ourselves and others in the process. Life is beautiful and is meant to be lived joyfully, but perfection does not exist therefore we must strive to live our life in excellence and give ourselves the best chance to succeed.

Toxic positivity refers to portraying yourself as being happy no matter what, and completely avoiding anything that may be viewed as negative. There are several aspects of today's culture that encourage a certain level of toxic positivity to be commonly found in society. One example of this is social media. While social media provides incredible tools for business and connections, it also leads many people to live a double life by giving them the opportunity to portray themselves differently than they really are. This may be in manipulation of their physical image, the illusion that they are financially more successful than they really are, or that they have a happy social life when in reality they are lonely and isolated. The sad part about this inauthenticity, is that in today's world, so much of a person's self-esteem and happiness are dictated by what other people think—by the amount of 'likes' or views they get. As more and more time is dedicated to social media, it becomes toxic because we allow it to control our lives—when in reality, we should control the time we spend on social media, and how it affects us.

A toxic mindset is the one that is pessimistic and stops growing, losing every battle before it's even fought. Many people sabotage themselves with their negative internal talk and find every possible reason to fail. A toxic mindset also lacks the ability to be mindful, self-aware, and grateful. Being mindful allows us to get through difficulties because we don't dwell on the past or worry about the future—we only have to exist in the here and now. Self-awareness allows people to break the cycle of focusing on negativity and weaknesses. Being thankful for what we have stops the negativity of how we see the world around us and of always wanting more from spreading like poison in our head. Not appreciating what we have leads us to focus on what we don't have and therefore trains our mind to focus on the bad or the negative.

A good way to deal with toxicity is to make time for the things that are important to you, starting by your health and moving into each and every area of your life that needs to be cleaned up. Most of us use the excuse that we don't have time which is also a toxic way of thinking. We all have time; there is time to check social media, right? Time is about priorities and about what you really want to do. It is important to replace the words 'have to' and 'need to' with 'want to' or 'get to.' You don't have to separate yourself from toxicity; You want to because it will make your life better. You don't need to do it—you get the opportunity to improve yourself.

Another way to deal with toxicity is to use strategic negativism, which refers to plan for the best—but prepare for the worse. It is not a pessimistic attitude, because it allows you to view possible problems with the intent of finding the solutions. It finds the negative only to create an action plan and turn it into something positive. A person with a great attitude finds solutions.

In all, I encourage you to pay attention to your life and to the environment you put yourself in. A toxic mindset—whether it is your own or coming from someone else—will slow you down, will prevent you from achieving goals, and will influence and stop you from becoming the best version of yourself.

Winner's Mentality

A winning mentality is when someone has enough self-belief in their abilities to know they can achieve anything they set their mind to do. A person with a winner's mentality is so focused on winning, that they see everything that happens as part of them winning—regardless of the outcome. This means they have the ability look at the things that are generally seen as losing and see them as part of their path to winning. This is the ultimate goal of a winner's mentality; you win even when you lose because you learned something that will make you better for next time.

In 2014, the Kansas City Royals lost game seven of the World Series in a dramatic fashion. As the organization's Mental Skills Coordinator, people often asked me what happened and why the team lost and almost every time people commented something along the lines of, 'I am sorry you guys lost'. Yes, it was unfortunate but definitely was nothing to be sorry about. The team battled and committed to winning with heart and passion and fell short of victory. Yes, the Royals lost but there was also a lot of winning that happened in the process. The feelings, emotions, and sensations of losing became a learning and growing experience which in turn made individuals and the team better and stronger.

Both winning and falling short of victory can create a feeling of positive stress. It is all about how you look at it and how you approach it. Winning at something makes you want to continue to work harder to get the same amazing feelings, emotions and sensations that come with winning. Losing on the other hand, can open your eyes by looking at the things that went wrong and finding ways to improve them. Losing is not necessarily a bad thing if it pushes you to work harder because in the process you will grow, you will continue to improve, and you will become better.

The following year, in 2015, the Kansas City Royals won the World Series. Since the team knew what it felt like to fail, and fall short of greatness, each and every player, staff and front office member learned from the experience, and wholeheartedly worked day in and day out to accomplish the goal. Failure or losing was only temporary, and it pushed everyone to work harder on the little things and therefore made everyone better and stronger.

Sometimes we have to fail a number of times before we eventually succeed. To put things in perspective, one of the world's greatest inventors, Thomas Edison failed thousands of times before inventing the light bulb. Imagine what it is like to lose or fail thousands of times at something and continuing to move forward with the same attitude, desire, and passion. Edison's famous quote is a testament to the attitude of a winner: "I have not failed, I just found 10,000 ways that won't work." This mentality allowed him to see the process of the invention as the win – not the actual win that came in the end.

Winners focus on the little things because they understand that little things become big things. They see that the little details that everyone seems to skip over are the things that make the difference. We all want things to happen fast, for success to come overnight. From birth, we wanted to walk before crawling, and wanted to run before walking. Somehow, throughout our life we are getting used to speed, to things happening very fast and if they are not happening quick enough, we quit and move on to something else. We want to go from zero to sixty miles per hour without understanding that there are steps, that there is a process. To get to sixty miles per hour, we have to go through 1 mph, 5mph, 20mph and so on until we get to sixty. This is where the 1% mentality comes in. The idea is to constantly improve yourself, your life, or whatever it is that you do, 1% at a time. To look at yourself in the mirror every night and know that regardless of how the day went or what happened throughout your day, that you are able to see the progress, even if it is little progress. If you make it a goal to improve just 1% each and every day over time you will have improved a very large amount and in turn, you will be better than you were before. One percent at a time.

Winning is not always about holding the trophy at the end, it is the mentality with which you approach each and every situation. You have the ability to get whatever you want out of each experience you have. Winners see opportunities where others see problems. Winners learn from their failure or mistakes and turn them into positive experiences. Winners don't lose, they just learn and because of that, they become better.

Win the Day

As mentioned in the previous section of a winner's mentality, winning is a decision you make. You have the unique ability to think about whatever you want to think about and if you think of winning only as holding that trophy at the end, you will miss all the opportunities for growth along the way.

Winning the day focuses on the short term, one day at a time, and it consists of doing three things that require absolutely no talent to accomplish. It is a personal decision of each individual to approach their day in a way in which they can successfully accomplish the following:

- Have fun.
- Be positive, and
- Give your ultimate best.

Based on science, research, and experience these three points are fundamental to the daily success in anyone's life. Contrary to popular perception, having fun doesn't mean to always be laughing and being loud, it means to enjoy oneself. Enjoyment is considered by many to be the most desirable of the seven universal emotions. Most people want and seek to enjoy everything they do, including enjoying their lives. However, a lot of people fail at truly enjoying what they do because they lived buried with tension and stress in their minds. They worry way too much about everything that they don't allow any room for enjoyment. Research shows that having fun and enjoying what you do relieves stress, leads to a healthier lifestyle, and 'speeds up' time. In addition, research proves that enjoyment is a fundamental requirement for true learning and for information to save in the long-term memory. Think about when you are doing something that truly amuses you, or something you truly enjoy doing. How quickly does time go by? Time seems to 'speed up' because you are so immersed into what you are doing that you lose perception of time.

Losing perception of time is a key factor in knowing whether or not you are truly enjoying yourself or what you are doing. During that process, when it seems like time is 'flying by' you are fully engaged, and there is meaning and purpose to what you are doing which in turn leads to the information of what you are doing to be saved in the long-term memory. Once the information is stored in the long-term memory, it will be there to be retrieved whenever you want. In your mind, go back to a time in school and think of your favorite subject. Chances are, even if you don't remember much about the class itself, you remember details like your teacher or the classroom because it was fun and enjoyable. You were probably looking forward to that class and it seemed as if the class went by really quickly. In the contrary, think about your worse subject, the class you didn't like, the class that seemed like it was never ending as if the clock moved in slow motion. Maybe you dreaded going to that class and therefore don't remember much about it. Fun and enjoyable information stores in the long-term memory and it is by different triggers or your own memory that you can retrieve whatever information you want from your past. Having fun and enjoying what you do can help you feel less overwhelmed by the stressors you face, which in turn can help you change your attitude towards the stressors so that you are less reactive when you experience stress.

You have the power and strength of mind to replace negativity with positivity and your body will adapt to however you decide to think. One way or another, the body will simply follow the orders given by your brain. This is how your mind is connected to your body. You think something either positive or negative and your body will react the same way. Lastly, the mentalities and examples described in this chapter are meant to strengthen your attitude. All you have to do is bring them to mind and act on them. Be aware of the mentalities, practice them consistently and little by little you will become mentally stronger because your attitude is going to be different.

Having fun, being positive, and giving your ultimate best on everything you do may seem like a very easy thing to do. However, it is challenging because all three are interconnected with one another. Regardless of whatever order they are placed, all three have a massive impact on one another. For example, as we mentioned before, life is not perfect and there is an infinite amount of possibilities for things to go wrong when we are doing something. When things are not going your way, it is very challenging to enjoy yourself, to be positive, and to continue giving your best. Science tells us that feelings and emotions cannot be controlled, and we all have them in a positive or negative way. However, with practice, you can learn to accept the feelings and emotions so that they do not control you and so your attitude becomes indestructible.

Focus and Concentration

To better understand how attitude, as well as the different approaches and mentalities explained in this Step, it is important to talk about the difference between focus and concentration. Most people misuse the words because they associate them as the same word. However, truth is, focus and concentration are two different words that mean completely different things. Focus refers to a main purpose or interest, a fact and being in tune with reality. Concentration is having your undivided attention on a single task or activity. Let's do a quick exercise. Stop reading for a bit, take 8 to 10 seconds to visually focus on this book and do not blink. What happened when you were staring, and you focused on this book? Did the book become blurry? Did you start seeing through it? Did the letters and words seem to start shifting from one place to another? Let's go over what happened.

As I asked you to do an exercise, you shifted from reading the book to a different task. The focus changed when I brought something else to your awareness (focusing on the book). At the same time, your mind knew that it is a fact that you are holding the book in your hands and that the book is real. During the 8-10 seconds you were focusing on the book, different thoughts or thinking patterns came into your mind. Maybe you were thinking about what the exercise was for? Or why the book was becoming blurry? And in a way, you were trying to control the thoughts and thinking patterns that were coming into your mind so that you could focus on the book. In the same manner as the previous exercise, stop reading for a bit, but this time concentrate in the book, blink all you want, and make sure all you are thinking about is concentrating in the book. Try it again. Repeat to yourself the words, 'I am concentrating in the book' over and over for the 8 to 10 seconds while you concentrate and stare at the book. What happened now? Did the book become blurry? Did other thoughts come into your mind? As you probably realized, the book did not get blurry because you were concentrating on one thought or thinking pattern. By repeating the words 'I am concentrating in the book' you did not allow any other thoughts to come into the mind.

Our attention span as human beings is very short, it is almost as long as the time it takes to blink, and up to 3 to 5 seconds for children and 8 to 15 seconds for adults. During that time, the mind is going to wander on its own unless we pre-occupy the mind with a single thinking pattern or task, such as 'concentrating in the book'. If you think about it from this perspective, the reason why you are able to watch a movie or read a book, is because you are constantly focusing and refocusing over and over again, and you are going in and out of concentration mode. The more you focus on something, whether it be a physical object or a thought, your attention is confined to a smaller and smaller area. When you concentrate the depth of your attention is greater.

When you concentrate, you put yourself exactly where you want to be at that specific moment in time. To prove this point, I always ask baseball players and spectators how long a baseball game is. Common knowledge is that most games last anywhere from 2 to 3 hours at the Major League level. Then I ask them, if it is possible to focus or concentrate for that amount of time? And the answer is always no. The truth is no one can focus nor concentrate for that long. Then I bring to their awareness the following concept: A baseball game is played in 18 minutes. That is the average amount of time in which the baseball is live so both players and spectators concentrate for very small periods of time, over and over. Concentration, in essence, happens pitch to pitch and in between pitches we fade away from concentration and start to focus on other things that come into the mind. When someone misses a play or a part of the game, it happens before the attention of the person shifted from the game to focusing on something else.

In the same manner, when you are watching a movie, and you miss something that happened during the movie, it happened because you went from concentrating on the movie to being aware and focusing on something else in your mind. Furthermore, the same thing happens with your negative attitude and emotions. They become the focus and therefore you miss the opportunity to concentrate on a new positive attitude or emotion. Practice, practice, and practice and you will be on your way to deal with whatever situation you are going through with the best possible attitude.

My encouragement to you is that you start implementing some of the mentalities discussed in this Step to Becoming the Best Version of Yourself and that you dedicate time to working on improving your attitude by just doing whatever it takes, because failure is not an option—as if your life depended on it. Just do it!

"It always seems impossible
until it is done."
Nelson Mandela

Exercise #6

Purpose: to change negative attitudes by replacing negative attitudes with positive ones.

Overall, your attitude as well as how you approach improving your attitude as outlined above, start with a decision you make in your mind. Be aware of the feelings, emotions, and sensations that come with the attitude you have had at any specific moment in time, allow them to take place for a short period of time and then redirect them in a different direction.

Attitudes are very much a process of awareness, focus, and concentration. If you have a bad attitude and are feeling sad for example, and you realize that the current attitude is detrimental to what you are trying to do or achieve, allow the sadness to take place. When you are ready to let it go, focus on a different attitude you want to have, like happiness. Once you replace a negative emotion with a positive emotion, you are practicing thought replacement. Subsequently, breathe correctly and relax for a minute so that you can submerge yourself into concentration and therefore, leave behind the previous negative attitude that was influencing your behavior.

With practice and repetition of the following steps you will be more likely to change negative attitudes and emotions more consistently.

1. Recognize the undesired attitude or emotion.
2. Focus on the new positive attitude or emotion you want to have.
3. Consistently repeat in your mind the new positive attitude or emotion you desire.
4. Breathe correctly and allow yourself to relax.
5. Your mind will begin to concentrate in the new desired attitude or emotion.

Step #7

To Becoming
The Best Version of Yourself

GOALS

Goals

"If you really want to do something,
you find a way...
if not, you find an excuse."
Jim Rohn

To say the least, this last Step to Becoming the Best Version of Yourself is going to be straightforward. To talk about goals, is to talk about something most people already know about and understand. Most of us have been dreaming about things and creating goals since we were kids. Some people reach their goals, while others fall short of the target. Why some people reach their goals and others don't, it is different for everyone.

I am going to approach this chapter in a different way, in a very challenging way with the idea of pushing you and your limits far beyond where they have been in the past. I want to push you to where the unattainable becomes a reality. Where goals do become true because that is what you want, period. No blaming, no complaining, no excuses simply getting to where you want to be—becoming what you want to become and achieving what you want to achieve because that is truly what you want. Science tells us that only 8 percent of people actually achieve their goals. A sad reality if you think about it. Actually, think about it for a second... Only 8 percent of people achieve their goals. It's a hard to comprehend because you and I both know that when you truly want to do something, and what I mean is, when you truly… truly… truly want to do something, you do it and nothing can or will stop you. To me, achieving goals is not about anything other than a decision you choose to make or a decision you choose to not make. Don't get me wrong, I understand that there are different variables that may impede you from accomplishing a dream or a goal, but the real question is, are you truly giving it your absolute best? Doing whatever it takes because failure is not an option? The mentalities and tools provided in this final Step to Becoming the Best Version of Yourself are intended to challenge you, to take you out of your comfort zone, to push you, and even to be make you be seen a little crazy because to achieve your goals, there has to be a little crazy in you.

There are many books and professionals out there that talk about how to create goals, about different goal achieving techniques, about the do's and don'ts. These experts will tell you to set goals in a specific way. Yes, I believe these topics are important and cannot be over-looked and I personally have used a lot of different goal setting tech-niques depending on who I am working with. I have used specific, measurable, attainable, realistic, and time-bound goals. In addition, I also have suggested to my clients to make their goals exciting and consistently to re-assess where they are at in their process of achiev-ing goals. However, as I mentioned before, it all boils down to one simple, yet very difficult thing to do—a decision. Do you really want to achieve your goals? or not?

Reasons People Don't Accomplish Goals

Let's go back to the research statement that only 8 percent of people achieve their goals. Except this time think about it the other way around; 92 percent of people don't achieve their goals. It is truly amazing to see what happens when you look at things from a different perspective. 92 percent of people don't achieve their goals! It is a ridiculous but true statement, and chances are, you have fallen into this percentile at one point or another in your life. Maybe even right now, you have dreams and goals you want to achieve, and you are not taking the necessary actions to get there.

As to the writing of this book, Google browser found 965,000,000 results in 0.35 seconds while searching for: 'the top reasons why people don't achieve goals.' Thus, so that you don't go crazy, I am going to simplify it for you by giving you my three reasons why people don't accomplish their goals. They are straight forward, and straight to the point:

- People quit before the fight begins,
- People quit during the fight, and
- People quit after the fight.

In other words, people convince themselves in their mind, or lack the motivation to start and give up before they even begin. People get motivated and they start the quest for their goals and give up in the process because it may be too hard. And lastly, people get to the end of their goal and don't get the results they expected and are too scared to either start all over again or continue moving forward.

Giving Up Before the Fight
*People give up because they convince themselves
to not start and they lack motivation*

A goal is the object of a person's ambition or effort. It is the destination of a journey. Goals are, in a way, our own unique ability to look into the future and wish, want, or desire something. Everyone in the world has dreams and creates goals in their mind. As we learned through Chevreul's pendulum, our bodies react to how we think, and truth is, we think a lot. The latest research estimates that the human mind thinks anywhere from 50,000 to 70,000 thoughts or thinking patterns per day, that is about 2100 to 3000 per hour, or about 35 to 50 per minute! So, next time you hear someone say that they are not thinking about anything, know that it is in fact almost impossible to not think anything.

For the purpose of this topic, I will focus on three parts of the mind that we use when we think: the conscious, the subconscious, and the reticular activating system. In short, the conscious mind is where you think, reason, make decisions, and exercise free will. The subconscious mind is a databank that stores your whole life in it, positive and negative experiences, beliefs, memories, and skills. Literally, it stores everything; anything you have ever seen, done or thought. The subconscious mind follows orders from the conscious mind and finds whatever necessary means to fulfill the order given by the conscious mind. Every day we are exposed to an overwhelming amount of information to which the reticular activating system acts as a filter to only allow information that is important to you into the subconscious mind.

The problem is that we are creatures of habit and learn by repetition, so thoughts and thinking patterns we constantly think about or dwell about will make it through the reticular activating system and therefore make it to our subconscious mind. At that point they become part of our belief system. Once the information is saved, the subconscious mind will do what it needs to do to make it happen, to make it a reality regardless of whether the information is positive or negative. Remember, about 80% of our thoughts and thinking patterns are negative (or geared towards the negative) so a lot of negativity is filtering through to the subconscious mind, becoming who we are and how we think. Our body is simply reacting to it. In a way, any thought or thinking pattern can turn into a goal because we think and overthink information over and over. That is why it is said that our mind is a goal creating machine. Through our thinking, it is setting conscious and subconscious goals constantly throughout our day and life.

Feelings, emotions, and sensations that lead people to give up before the fight begins, include:

- Not having energy,
- Problems,
- Tension,
- Stress,
- Anxiety,
- Depression,
- Uncertainty,
- Doubt,
- Fear, and
- Bad choices.

Most people overthink information which leads the body to become paralyzed through a process called 'paralysis by analysis.' It is through constant repetition of our thinking patterns and overthinking, that we find a way to convince ourselves to not start or to not do something. Our negative internal conversations lead us to lack the motivation we need to accomplish our goals. We find whatever excuse we can come up with to not close the gap between where we are and where we want to be.

Fortunately, thanks to neuroplasticity, we know that the brain has the ability to reorganize itself by forming new neural connections and therefore the brain can be rewired with new information. When we think, we create goals, and the purpose of goals is to create cognitive dissonance—which occurs when conflicting thoughts, beliefs, or attitudes create dissatisfaction in the brain—leading the subconscious mind to do what it needs to do to reduce the conflict and make it happen. Our unique ability to look into the future creates constant goals and dissatisfaction in ourselves. We look at where we are in life and pursuantly think of where we want to be, or we look at what we don't have and think of what we want to have in our life. Therefore, we are constantly creating goal after goal in our minds and don't do anything to change our life. If you don't like where you are in life, your present status, or your current situation, it is because you have been creating that negative goal in a subconscious way. You are in a way, achieving the goal of not starting to achieve your goal.

If you give up on chasing your dreams or your goals before you even begin, you will always be where you are. You will never start and therefore you will always have the same poor mentality, the same status, financial situation, and you will stay in the emotional place you are today. You will have the same job, the same stress, anxiety, and depression. Same problem, drama, pain, or same whatever word you want to add. Just remember, if you don't start, you will never know what you can do or how far you can go.

In baseball terms, if you give up before you walk up to home plate because the pitcher is throwing hard or you are afraid, you will never get to experience the feeling of standing in the box. You will never know what it is like to hit the ball because you aren't even trying it. You will never know if you can hit the ball because you are too afraid to step in the box. My question to you is, do you want to step in the box? Do you want to achieve your goals?

It is your decision!

Giving Up During the Fight
People give up because along the way
things get too hard or complicated

In 2005, one of my best friends Francisco Rodriguez from Mexicali, Mexico was a top candidate for Rookie of the Year in the Mexican Pacific League. Due to his incredible performance and individual achievements during the Winter, the Anaheim Angels signed him to play in the minor leagues and therefore he started his journey to achieving his goal of making it to the big leagues. From the minute we met at the hotel in Phoenix, Arizona we developed an instant connection and so we ended up rooming together through our journey in the minor leagues. During his first year of professional baseball in 2006, which was my second, we both headed to Rancho Cucamonga, California. At that time, the Quakes were the class Single A Advanced team of the Anaheim Angels.

Paco, as I call him, was a starting pitcher at the time and his first year of professional baseball was the worst year of his career—performance-wise. He finished the year with 5 wins and 13 losses and after each start he had, he would come home completely defeated and wanting to quit. It was a rough year to say the least. He started the season with 0 wins and 5 losses, and nothing seemed to go his way. I clearly remember how after each game he pitched, he would come home and literally pack his bags. We argued and argued day after day and with curse words I'd yelled at him time after time telling him that he was not going to go anywhere, that he wasn't going to quit. In his mind, Paco wanted to go back to Mexico where he was comfortable, where people could understand him because at that time, Paco didn't speak English. In his mind, playing in Mexico seemed to be the best option at the time; more pay, better living conditions, and a better environment. His first year in the United States, Paco led the league in losses with 13 and literally went through hell on the field, and in his mind. He felt like the whole 6-month season was nothing but failure.

Fast-forward 4 years, to April 13th, 2010. While rooming together in Triple A, we came back to the room after a day game and the hotel phone was flashing; there was a voice message. I listened to the message and informed Paco that it was the Assistant General Manager saying that he needed to speak to him immediately. When a front office person is looking for you, it is usually not good news. Paco was nervous, shaking, and visibly fearful as to expecting the worst possible news—getting released. But it was amazing to see first-hand how nerves, and fear turned into tears of joy and happiness as that day, Paco became the 111th Mexican-born player to ever make it to the Major Leagues.

Paco's story and journey to success is an example of what all of us go through in life when looking to achieve our goals. We are going to go through:

- Ups and downs,
- We are going to face challenges and difficulties,

- We are going to experience setbacks,
- Tension,
- Stress,
- Problems,
- Limitations,
- Fears,
- Roadblocks, and
- We may even feel like we are going through hell.

Notice I used the word 'through' hell. That means we are going to go t-h-r-o-u-g-h- it, not stay there. Our mind might tell us to give up, or to quit, but just because things get too hard along the way doesn't mean we need to stop. In fact, it means we are getting closer to our goal and we just need to continue to push forward through the challenges, fears, and roadblocks. That evening, April 13th, 2010, Paco hugged me with tears in his eyes and said "Thank you! This would have never happened if you let me quit."

If you give up on chasing your dreams or your goals in the middle of your journey, you will always wonder what could have happened if you pushed yourself through to the end. Yes, you will have accomplished certain feats along the way, feel somewhat good about yourself because you tried, but you will always wonder the 'what if'. Ultimately deep in your mind, you will always know that you are a quitter and that you quit simply because it got too hard. Let me tell you something, no one said the goals you set would be easy. No goal is ever achieved without going through obstacles—but with a strong mentality and by applying the techniques in this book, you can finish the fight no matter what difficulties and hardships come your way. The only limitation you have is in your mind.

In baseball terms, if you walk away in the middle of the at bat because you have two strikes and you are afraid of striking out, you will always wonder what could have been. If you quit and don't finish the at bat, you will never get a hit because you quit during the process. My question to you is, do you want to finish the at bat? Do you want to pursue your goals to the end?

It is your decision!

Giving up After the Fight
People give up after achieving goals because
there is no drive to go on, no matter what happens

On September 8th, 2008, my long-time goal of reaching the Major Leagues became a reality. On that night, I became the 17,061st player in the history of the game to reach the Major Leagues. To give you an idea of how rare it is to actually achieve that dream, let's look at the most recent statistics. According to the Register Players Encyclopedia, in February 2019 there was 310,903 players in history recorded to have ever played minor league baseball. But as of the same month, only 19,429 players had ever had the opportunity to play at the Major League Level. That is a 6.25% success rate.

It is commonly known and said that in professional baseball the 'easy' part is to make it to the Majors (…easy considering only 6.25% of players who sign a professional contract will ever play a game in the Major Leagues) but that the 'hard' part is to stay long enough to make a career out of baseball. Although there is no clear statistic, it is said that only about 0.07% of the 6.25% of players that get to the big leagues stay long enough to make a career out of the game. That is only about 1360 players at the time that I am writing this book.

My stint in the Major Leagues was anything but easy. I was there for just under a year of Major League service. A Major League Season consists of 183 days and each day spent on the active roster or injured list earns the player a day of service. A player is deemed to have reached one year of service upon accruing 172 days in any given year. Over three seasons, 2008 and 2009 on the active roster, and 2011 in the injured list, I accumulated just under one year of service. I am a part of the statistic. A part of the 0.07% that didn't stay long enough in the big leagues to make a career of the game.

In 2009, I was sent back down to the minor leagues where I suffered my first injury during the first few weeks of the Triple A season; a torn ligament in my left wrist. I was told by the doctors that I was out for the season. This was the first instance in my life where I consciously experienced the power of the mind. I got to the big leagues in 2008, back down to the minors in 2009 and was told I was done for the year. But in my mind, there was no way in hell I was done; and I wasn't going to settle. I could have easily settled and accepted the fact that I was hurt and done for the year. However, it was the opposite, I wanted to get back to the big leagues and nothing was going to stop me. I worked diligently on my physical body, my therapy, and my mind. I did whatever I had to do, without blaming, without complaining, and without making excuses. I simply just did what I had to do to accomplish my goal of getting back as soon as possible. I made a plan, changed my limiting beliefs, and changed meal plans. I even changed habits, replaced friends, and adapted to new routines. I visualized getting healthy. Overall, I changed my mentality. I committed 100% to overcome every obstacle in my life and my mind. I eliminated all the things that were stopping me from becoming a better person and player. I changed and transformed my life and moved forward except this time, stronger. I looked at my injury and my life, and I didn't like what I saw, I didn't like where I was, so I grabbed the problems and took action to turn them into solutions. It was a difficult and challenging time; after accomplishing my goal of getting to the Big Leagues, I was knocked down with an injury. What was I supposed to do? Just sit tight and wait for things to happen on their own? That's not who I am. I make things happen. So, I got back up and started fighting again with a new goal—to make it back to the big leagues that same year. Aside from changing the numerous areas in my life mentioned above, I rehabbed my wrist multiple times a day, with the trainers and at home, strengthening and doing pool exercises. I also took care of my wrist, followed the rules, and didn't do anything I wasn't supposed to do. I committed myself and gave my absolute best on everything I did from the rehab process to allowing my wrist to heal and everything in between.

In a few words, I relentlessly worked my ass off even after I was told I was out for the season. Five months of complete devotion to improving myself, while everyone else thought I was done for the year. At first, I was in a cast and limited to what I could do with my hand, but I continued working on other areas like my physical shape and my mind. Day after day, progressions started to happen, and each day I could do more and more. When the cast was completely removed, my body was in the best shape of my life, my mind was strong, and to everyone's surprise, my wrist after being in a cast for a couple of months, was healthy and strong. At that time, because of how my wrist had healed, the rehab process changed. There was now a slight possibility of me being able to swing the bat and even a smaller chance of me playing on the field—but I continued with the same plan and same goal of coming back the same year. Long story short, in mid-August of 2009, I went back to play in Triple A and a few weeks later, I was back in the big leagues.

The following two years, I got hurt again. In 2010 I had a tear in the ulnar collateral ligament (known in baseball as the Tommy John injury) and was out for the year. In 2011, I tore my internal and external obliques and was out for 5 months. These were two difficult years as I battled depression in 2010, and anxiety in 2011 both of which limited me to achieve more baseball related goals. However, I invested and worked on myself as I constantly do and set new goals outside of baseball—goals for my career and for my life. I always set very high goals because the expectations I have for myself are very high and even when I don't achieve all of my goals, the learning, growth, and experience that I take from each goal, makes me better and stronger—and thus, prepares me for the next goal. It is who I am, I devote myself completely to my goals and to what I do no matter what happens. If something doesn't pan out the way I want it, or expect it, I re-structure it and continue to move forward with a whatever it takes mindset. Giving up is not an option. And failing is not an option because if I fail, I find a new way, a new road, or a new path but always pushing forward and always following my goals.

My entire life, probably just like your life, I have created goals. Over the years, I have achieved some of those goals, and failed at others. But the most important thing I would like for you to learn from this section is that I am always working on new ones. As I mentioned before, when I set goals, I shoot for the stars because I know what I am capable of. I know and understand that the only thing that is stopping and limiting me from achieving my goals, is my own mind. So, I work on myself each and every day to control my mind and actions and thus, give myself the best possible chance to conquer the mission I set out to complete. In the same way, the only thing stopping you from being invincible and from achieving your goals is the limiting beliefs you set in your mind. Norman Vincent

Peale said, 'Shoot for the moon. Even if you miss, you'll land among the stars.' When you set a high goal and get knocked down, get back up with a new goal and move towards it every single day. I guarantee you one thing, even if you don't get to the moon, you will end up in the stars, meaning you will end up in a different place with new ideas, opportunities and possibilities. At the same time, you will have learned and grown, and therefore be ready for your new conquest because you have become better than before.

If you find yourself in a situation where you have met your goal— you achieved what you set out to—but once you got there, you wanted or expected something different, you are not alone. So many people can relate to this. However, in that moment of dissatisfaction, if you don't start a new goal, you will never succeed at the overall journey of life.

Resiliency is a crucial key in accomplishing whatever goals you have. When you don't get the results you want or expect, and are knocked down, you assess the situation, you recover and get back up to do it all over again because that is who you are. You create a new plan but this time, you do it better because you are stronger. You are mentally strong to achieve any goal you set in your mind simply because nothing can or will stop you. Failure or the culmination of a goal doesn't mean you are done; it means you take the learning and find new ways to accomplish something else. Failure only makes you better and stronger. Finishing a goal and not feeling satisfied with the result you got will only build you up and make you better for the next goal.

In baseball terms, if you never want to hit again because you struck out and you are afraid of striking out again, you will never succeed. You will always limit yourself and will never know what you are capable of. If you stop, you will never accomplish the new goal, you will never make it to the big leagues. My question to you is, do you want to step in the box again after striking out? Do you want to make new goals when you finish a goal and feel unsatisfied?

It is your decision!

Ways to Accomplish Goals

Deepak Chopra once said, "Perception is the selective act of attention and interpretation." This book is filled with different theories, ideals, concepts and the principles I teach people that change the perception of their reality and to become mentally stronger.

By definition, a mentally strong person is someone who can handle whatever situation they are in with calm and ease. They are in control of their mind and persevere because they know they can do anything. No matter how much stress is presented, the circumstance, or what is happening, this person can rely on their mental strength to handle his or her business and let go of whatever is not working for them.

Up until now, each step of Mentally Strong was designed to prepare you to get to this point. Through the application of each of the concepts you will become a mental ninja. The following are the final three pieces of the puzzle. As a mentally strong person, you just don't quit in the pursuance of your goals. However, when your mind tells you to quit before the fight, during the fight or after the fight, you respond by applying one or all of the next concepts: internal motivation, staying in the present, and using perspective.

Internal Motivation

What motivates people in life is a difficult question to answer because it is personal, and different for everyone. There are my motivational theories that give us information, possibilities, and ideas to prove different points. The mentalities I am going to explain originate from different theories but are more than anything my own principles, and my way to motivate people. They might seem harsh and straight to the point but in my experience, they give people the motivation needed to accomplish their goals.

In the 3rd Step to Becoming the Best Version of Yourself, you learned about the power of asking questions... the right questions. Questions that go deep into the subconscious mind and override the negative thinking patterns that come into the mind throughout the process of accomplishing any goal. Accomplishing goals requires direction, a plan, and effort.

- **When there is a lack of internal motivation, the first question to ask yourself is, how bad do I want it?** Your answer to this question will give you direction. If you want it, great, now you know that. If you don't, then move on to the next goal.
- **The second question to ask yourself is, what am I going to do about it?** Your answer to this question will give you a work plan. The plan may require guidance, a mentor, or help. Put your ego aside, seek the help you need and always move towards the goal. Put the plan into action, otherwise your goal is just hallucination.
- **Lastly, ask yourself, is that the best I can do?** Your answer will let you know your effort level. If your goal is meaningful enough to you, your effort level should be nothing less than your absolute best. Do what you need to do to make it

happen. Go after your goal with everything you've got, but always allow your ethical compass guide you. Do it right, or don't do it at all.

Motivation comes through inspiration. Passive inspiration happens when you are motivated by a video, movie, or a book and you become convinced that it was just what you needed to turn your life around. Passive inspiration is when you take someone else's success story as inspiration. You start off motivated, but as days or weeks go by, your motivation fades away and you go back to your old patterns. You're back to reality and unmotivated.

Active inspiration on the other hand, happens when the motivation comes from you—from within. It comes from your mind, heart, and soul. You create it, you produce it, you experiment with it and it jump-starts you and gets you going. It puts you in motion because you're making it happen.

Isaac Newton's first law of motion states that 'an object at rest stays at rest and an object in motion stays in motion.' If you roll a baseball, it will continue to roll until it comes to rest, then it will stay at rest until something or someone rolls the baseball again. Our goals work the same way than the first law of motion. If you don't move towards your goals, your goals will remain where they are—far away from you. If you want to get up earlier for example, as soon as your alarm goes off, your mind will tell you it's easier to stay in bed a little longer; but just get up! Get going and your body will continue to move. It is that simple. The first thing you have to do is start. Then, once you get going you must continue to put in the work to move in the direction of your goal. Not a little later, or tomorrow, it has to be right now. Stop making excuses and just do it.

Similarly, the intrinsic and extrinsic motivational theory talks about internal and external factors that give you a push and drive you to achieve something. Internal refers to factors inside of you, like your passion and joy. It differs from passive inspiration because internal factors are about you and not someone else. Motivation from videos, books, and movies fades away because we fail at relating it and applying it to ourselves. External factors refer to external rewards, like money, or recognition but external factors that are materialistic also can fade away because physical things can be taken away from us at any given moment. Thus, this is where the 'watch me' mentality was born. For better external motivation use a person. We all have someone in our lives that has made us feel less, incompetent, or stupid. Someone who told us we weren't good enough; that we couldn't do it. The 'watch me' mentality uses that person as your motivation. When your mind is telling you to give up, or to not do something, bring that person to mind and prove that person wrong. The 'watch me' mentality says, 'I am getting it done because you don't think I can'. This mentality is an incredibly powerful motivator because it hits you where it hurts—in your ego. You don't think I can run a marathon? Watch me. This mentality lights a fire inside of you and turns you on.

You cannot watch television if you don't turn it on. It is that simple, you want any electronic device to work, you have to turn it on. Logically, our body is not electronic, but our mind understands that for anything to work, it needs to be turned on. For that reason, you have to turn your motivation on; you have to turn yourself on. Physically with your index finger touch a part of your body as you would to turn any electronic. As you are turning yourself on, mentally repeat to yourself 'I am on, let's go!' Repeat this process many times throughout the day or whenever you want to turn yourself on. Your mind is going to make the connection that every time you touch that part of your body with your index finger, you are turning yourself on and it is go time. It will turn into an anchor. Anchors are a very powerful physical self-starter for motivation. The more you practice this, the better it is going to work. If you never use it, it will slowly go away. You have the power in you, physically and mentally to turn yourself on and move in the direction of your goals any time you want.

Every single success story in the history of the world started with motivation and a goal. It began with the willingness and desire to accomplish something. Success doesn't happen on its own, you have to make it happen.

- Stop making excuses as to why you can't achieve your goals.
- Motivate yourself by asking yourself questions and start moving in the direction of your goals.
- Inspire yourself from within and turn on that fire inside of you.
- Prove people wrong because you can do anything you set your mind to do.
- Believe in yourself, because no one is going to believe in you more than your own self.
- Achieve your goals because that is the only option you have.
- Stop comparing yourself to others and focus on you—on your life, your goals, and on making sure each day, you write your own success story.
- Remember, success is a reflection of your attitude and your work-ethic.

"Dream it, believe it, achieve it."
Unknown

Staying in the Present

Time as a unit of measurement is constant—always moves forward and never backward. Time is also one of the biggest excuses we use as individuals when we say, I don't have time. We all have time; our day is always going to be 24 hours. What we do with the time we have, is a different story. How much time we spent thinking about the past, the present, and the future is a constant debate that will continue to puzzle scientist for years. Some researchers have proposed that the average human being spends on average about 70 percent of their thinking time in the past, 10 percent in the present and 20 percent in the future. While others believe that we spend more time in the future than in the past. However, the one thing most researchers agree on is in regard to how little time human beings actually spend thinking and taking action in the present moment. As with most research, the numbers are just statistics and they are not definite. The numbers may fluctuate from one person to another. But think about it for a second and ask yourself the question, where do I spend most of my time? Are you thinking mostly in the past, the present, or the future?

Whether you spend more time thinking about the past or the future makes no difference at all, the point is the little amount of time you spend thinking and acting in the present. When the mind is thinking about the past it is thinking in terms of certainty. You know for certain the things that happened or didn't happen, and you add your feeling, emotions, and sensations to those thinking patterns. In the present, your mind thinks in terms of probability; your mind calculates the chances of something happening down the road. In the future, your mind is all about possibilities, will it happen or not? Let me remind you, that the average human being thinks in a negative way or geared towards negativity about 80% of the times. Chances are, whether you are thinking of the past, present, or future, you will think of that moment in a negative way. You will dwell on the past, worry about the future, and therefore forget to live in the present.

In order for you to be in the present moment more consistently you have to start by cleaning up your life. There is an overwhelming amount of information in your brain that shouldn't be there and cleaning up processes, habits, and routines in your life will allow you to stop thinking about that unnecessary information. If you want a better life, start replacing habits, negativity, and friends. Get rid of the toxicity of your life, including relationships that are bringing you down. You don't need them in your life, they are only slowing you down and causing you to be like them. Mentally strong people are positive outliers—people who are different from all other members. If you want to achieve your goals and be successful, separate from the rest in a good way; be different, be unstoppable.

From a mental perspective, energy, attention, and focus all-together work the same way. Your energy goes, where your attention goes, and where your attention goes, you focus on that. All three words can be interchanged in whatever order but regardless, they lead to the same idea. If you focus on the past, that is where your attention and energy will go. If you are paying too much attention to a problem in the present, that is where your energy and your focus will go. Likewise, if you cannot stop thinking of the future, your focus, attention, and energy will also go there.

My advice is to live your life in short periods of time so that you can live and enjoy the present moment more consistently. Control what you can control. Replace the time you spend thinking about the past or the future and make the decision to think of your present. If you are a person that thinks for say, 50 percent of the time in the future, and 25 percent in the past and present, replace the future percentage with the present percentage and think 50 percent on the present and 25 percent on the future. The past is only good for two reasons: to learn from it, and to remember good things that happened; not to dwell on it. Thinking of the future is important because it allows you to create goals, but you have to spend most of your time in the present time. The past is gone, and the future hasn't happened yet. When you make the absolute most of your present, I guarantee you your future will improve.

To live your life in short periods of time means to bring your attention to what is in front of you, and to what you can control. The only moment in time you can control is the present—the right now. I call this the 'draw a line' mentality, which requires awareness to recognize what's happening in that specific moment. Literally, draw an imaginary line with your index finger at arm's length. That imaginary line becomes your target. The second you cross that imaginary line, you leave the past behind you; the behavior, or attitude that you had, and you cross with a new better attitude and behavior. In the same manner, you can use this mentality to achieve goals, just focus on what is in front of you, you don't have to live the whole day at once. Focus on the next five minutes, or the next thirty seconds if necessary. The average adult is awake for about 15 to 16 hours a day and if you are overwhelmed, that can be too long. Instead of looking at the 15-16 hours ahead of you, live your day one hour at a time 15 or 16 times. Or split the next hour into twelve five-minute segments. On an extremely difficult or painful day, you may have to live just five seconds at a time and that is okay because you can control the next 5 seconds. Live your life in short periods of time so that you can control every aspect of your life in the present moment. Remember, for a few seconds, you can be in total control of your mind and can do anything you want.

When I lived in Phoenix, Arizona, my kids started to develop fears to scorpions. Wrongfully, I talked a lot about scorpions and asked my kids to be careful. Overtime, I instilled a fear in them about scorpions. On a given day, I found a fairly sized dead scorpion in the yard. I asked one of my sons to hold it and he refused. I talked to him for a few minutes and told him 'for 10 seconds you can do, and you can be anything you want. Just for 10 seconds, and not a second more. Remember you can do anything!' At age 5, my son discovered the power of affirmations, the power of I am, I do, and I can. As mentioned before in the 5th Step to Becoming the Best Version of Yourself, affirmations are incredibly powerful because they override our negative thinking patterns. My son held the scorpion with his fingers for 10 seconds, just enough time for me to take a picture. 'I am brave because I did it. I can do anything like Superman, Daddy.' he responded. You too can do absolutely anything you want for a short period of time. You can be anyone you want for a few minutes or even just a few seconds. Sometimes you have to turn yourself into a superhero in your mind for just enough time to accomplish your goals. Use the 10 second rule and the superhero mentality at will, and you too will discover that for a short period of time, you can be the best version of yourself.

- Clean up your life and be mindful of what is happening in the present moment. It is fundamental to having a strong mindset.
- Allow your thoughts and emotions to come and go without judgement.
- Breathe correctly, slow yourself down and think of the best possible way to come back to the present time.

- Draw a line for your past and cross it to a better present and your future will improve.
- Live in short periods of time and be a superhero—and remember that for 10 seconds, you can do and be anyone you want to be. Then, do it over and over again until it becomes who you are all the time. It may be challenging at first, but with practice and repetition you will do it because it is who you are.
- Live in the present and when you are there, carpe diem—urge yourself to make the most of the present moment.

"Today is the tomorrow you worried about yesterday."
Dale Carnagie

Perspective

Who are you? You are a human being, and as a person, you are created and recreated with the purpose of understanding yourself. You are designed to learn and grow by using the brain you were given to expand your thinking mind. You have the ability to communicate systematically. You take in information through your five senses and interpret that information in whatever way you want. You interpret life based on your values, beliefs, attitudes, experiences, memories, and how you process that information. You make your own decisions and bear the consequences for them. You are a creature of habit and 90 to 95 percent of your life is driven by your subconscious mind. You are what you think and what you think, is what you do. What is your purpose? To survive. The purpose of all life species is survival and to survive in this world as a human being, you have to be mentally strong so that you can go through all the curveballs life is going to throw at you.

Many people, reporters, and different media outlets have asked me to define what being mentally strong means to me in one word. My answer is always the same: perspective. Perspective is a particular attitude toward something, or the way of regarding something. It is an idea, an angle, a point of view; your own point of view. It doesn't mean you are right, or you are wrong. It is simply the way you look and think of something; it is your truth and your reality in that moment. Perspective, in a sense, is similar to the self-fulfilling prophecy because whatever you believe in, you are right—it is your way of looking at things and the way you think. Your initial perspective is unique to you until you think differently and change your perspective. The leading cause of all arguments in life is, in a way, a difference in perspectives. People passionately talk about how they see things and think about things, and if it's different than yours, it often leads to disagreement. Just a simple difference of opinion can turn into an argument or a problem—you are right, and they are wrong and vice versa. The trouble with this approach is that it's not necessarily true. In life, there are few things that are absolutely right or wrong. If you are aware and truly understand the power of perspective, you remain in control and accept people's comments even if you don't agree. What is the point of an argument anyways? To prove you are right? A mentally strong person doesn't care if he or she is right or wrong—they have perspective to assess and control the situation. If you agree or disagree, who cares—take the information and move on. Think about it like this. Your mind and body are connected, and you have the ability to see things from any perspective you want, so arguments and drama are only going to affect you negatively. Your perspective is your perception, and yours alone. Your perception is what is going on in your individual inner world. If you don't control your inner world, your inner world is going to control you.

Perspective is important when working towards achieving goals, because you have to have the ability to think outside the box. Thinking outside the box is not just a phrase. It is about the ability to use perspective to see the whole picture and see goals or problems in a different way to expand your horizon in a more innovative way. It is about understanding where you are, where you want to go, and thinking about it in a way you have never thought of before. To achieve true perspective, you need to stop being a know-it-all because the truth is, you don't know it all. Your way is not always the best way and if you want to be successful you have to be willing and able to learn, take advice, and try different things.

- Expand on what you know by learning about new things outside of your area of expertise.
- Talk to people and hear what they have to say. Like I said before, you don't have to agree but accepting what they have to say may come in handy later on.
- Even take advice from children, their perspective on things is always unique and amazing.
- Turn things upside down, not just physically but also in your mind; imagine situations as if you were on the other side of things. Put yourself on someone else's shoes.
- And my favorite way of thinking outside the box: plan backwards. Create your goal and instead of planning how you are going to get there, see yourself accomplishing the goal and think of the steps that it took to get there backwards until you get to where you are now. If achieving your goal for example required 10 steps, what was the ninth step, and the eighth

and all the way down to when you began. That is thinking outside the box, a different perspective that might give you different ways of doing things and accomplish your goals.

Throughout this book, I meticulously described and explained each of the topics with the hope that you could learn something you didn't know before. In the process, you grew and are now more aware of what it takes to become mentally strong and for that reason, you are better than before. This book focused one hundred percent on *you* and what *you* can control—what you think about, the images in your mind, and your actions. C. Wright Mills, in his book The Sociological Imagination, provides another perspective. Mills encourages people to stop focusing only on themselves and to look at the wider landscape of society. Mills believed that every problem you face has its roots in society. The struggles you face every day are not unique to you, there are probably thousands of people struggling the same way you are. Sociological imagination can be applied to any behavior, for instance, drinking soda can be seen by some people as incredible satisfaction, while someone else might see it as too much sugar. It can be seen as a ritual in some cultures while it's seen as an addiction by other people. Social imagination happens when your perspective shifts from that of your own and you start thinking about other issues, matters, or activities. Mills view is neither right nor wrong, it only provides a completely different perspective on the way you can look at things.

The principles and steps of this book were designed and placed in a specific order for you to gradually start becoming mentally stronger. From my professional perspective, they are the fundamental keys to developing a stronger mindset. It doesn't mean that my way is right or wrong; what truly matters is what you believe, how you interpret it, and whether or not you are willing to experiment with it. But in my experience, having worked individually with hundreds of athletes, people, organizations, and businesses, these 7 Steps to Becoming the Best Version of Yourself have been a framework and structure to become mentally strong and forever be transformed.

Life is what you make of it, and so is this book. Who you are and who you want to be is one hundred percent up to you, it is your decision!

"The right perspective makes the impossible possible."
Unknown

Final Words

Today, we live in a world fueled by instant gratification. Children and adults alike are getting used to the idea that we don't have to work hard to gain a reward. The general perception is that success is an easy goal to accomplish. Life is beautiful, but it is by no means easy. We are overwhelmed with information, technology, and stress. In order for us to make it through the temptation, challenges, and ups and downs of life, we have to work hard. We have to work really hard. It boils down to our ability to be very strict on ourselves, our mentality, and our goals. We have to be mentally strong.

Always remember:

- You are in control of everything you think about, everything you see in your mind, and all the actions and behaviors you exert.
- You make the decisions. Be aware of how you think and be more positive.
- Take responsibility for your life and communicate effectively with yourself and others.
- Deal with your stress by taking care of the stressors.
- Relax consistently so you can be in control of your body and have a 'I am just going to do whatever it takes because failure

is not an option' mentality to achieve each and every one of your goals.

You are who you are because you want to be the way you are; if you want more and want to become better, start by prioritizing what is important in your life. Give yourself the best opportunity to succeed by becoming the best version of yourself—everyday. And take action to change—it is your decision! My best to you always.

"I am, I do, I can."
Freddy Sandoval

Appendix

Myers Briggs Type Indicator

The Myers Briggs Type Indicator is a self-report inventory designed to identify a person's personality type, strengths, and preferences. According to the Myers & Briggs Foundation, the essence of the theory is that much seemingly random variation in the behavior is actually quite orderly and consistent, being due to the basic differences in the way individuals prefer to use their perception and judgement.

The MBTI instrument has been researched hundreds of times in different studies over the last 40 years and the instrument has been proven to be valid and reliable. The goal of knowing about your personality type is to help you understand and appreciate the normal differences between people. There is no perfect type and no type is better than another. The instrument does not measure trait, ability, or character, it is designed to sort for preferences in perception by Extraversion-Introversion, Sensing-Intuitive, Thinking-Feelings, and Judging-Perceiving.

For information on taking the 93-question assessment and to obtain your results please visit www.mbti.org or contact me directly on www.thechoicetobelieve.com

Understanding of the Type Concepts

Extraversion (E)	Introversion (I)
Oriented in the outer world.	Oriented in the inner world
Focusing on people and things	Focusing on ideas, inner
Active	impressions
Using trial and error with	Reflective
confidence	Considering deeply before acting
Scanning the environment for	Finding stimulation inwardly
stimulation	

Sensing Perception (S)	Intuitive Perception (N)
Perceiving with the five senses	Perceiving with memory and
Attending to practical and factual	associations
details	Seeing patterns and meanings
In touch with the physical realities	Seeing possibilities
Attending to the present moment	Projecting possibilities for the
Confining attention to what is said	future
& done	Imagining, "reading between the
Seeing "little things" in everyday	lines"
life	Looking for the big picture
Attending to "step-by-step"	Having hunches, "ideas out of
experience	nowhere"
Letting "the eyes tell the mind"	Letting "the mind tell the eyes"

Thinking Judgement (T)	Feeling Judgement (F)
Using logical analysis	Applying personal priorities
Using objective and personal	Weighing human values and
criteria	motives, my own
Drawing cause and effect	and others
relationships	Appreciating
Being firm-minded	Valuing warmth in relationships
Prizing logical order	Prizing harmony
Being skeptical	trusting

Judging (J)	Perceiving (P)
Using thinking of feeling	Using sensing or intuitive
judgement	perception
outwardly	outwardly
Deciding and planning	Taking in information
Organizing and scheduling	Adapting and changing
Controlling and regulating	Curious and interested
Goal oriented	Open-minded
Wanting closure, even when data	Resisting closure to obtain more
are	data
incomplete	

16 Different Personality Types

Introverted Types

ISTJ	ISFJ	INFJ	INTJ
Quietly systematic. Factual. Organized. Logical. Detailed. Conscientious. Analytical. Stable. Responsible. Pragmatic. Critical. Conservative. Decisive. Concrete. Efficient.	Quiet. Warm. Factual. Sympathetic. Detailed. Dependable. Organized. Thorough. Conscientious. Systematic. Stable. Conservative. Realistic. Caring. Practical. Helpful.	Vision and meaning oriented. Quietly intense. Insightful. Creative. Sensitive. Seeks harmony, growth. Serious. Loves language, symbols. Persevering. Inspiring.	Vision oriented. Quietly innovative. Insightful. Conceptual. Logical. Seeks understanding. Critical. Decisive. Independent. Determined. Pursues competence, improvement.
ISTP	**ISFP**	**INFP**	**INTP**
Logical. Quietly analytical. Practical. Adaptable. Curious. Cool. Observer. Problem-solver. Exact. Realistic. Troubleshooter. Hands-on. Variety Adventurous. Independent.	Gentle. Quietly caring. Compassionate. Adaptable. Modest. Aesthetic. Idealistic. Observant. Loyal. Helpful. Realistic. Patient with details. Spontaneous. Joy in action.	Deep-felt valuing. Quietly caring. Compassionate. Pursues meaning, harmony. Creative. Idealistic. Empathetic helpers. Inquisitive. Enjoys ideas, language, writing. Independent. Adaptable.	Logical. Conceptual. Analytical. Objective. detached. Critical. Ingenious. Complex. Intellectually curious. Loves ideas. Pursues understanding. Questioning. Adaptable. Independent.

Extroverted Types

ESTP	ESFP	ENFP	ENTP
Excitement seeking. Active. Pragmatic. Direct. Easygoing. Observant. Concrete. Realistic. Adaptable. Efficient. Analytical. Troubleshooter. Spontaneous. Adventurous. Experiential.	Energetic. Sociable. Practical. Friendly. Caring. Expressive. Open. Enthusiastic. Excitement seeking. Spontaneous. Resourceful. Adaptable. Observant. Hands-on. Generous. Fun-loving.	Enthusiastic. Imaginative. Energetic. Creative. Warm. Future-oriented. Individualistic. Insightful. Caring. Optimistic. Possibility focused. Open. Novelty seeking. Spontaneous. Playful.	Energetic. Inventive. Enthusiastic. Abstract. Logical. Theoretical. Analytical. Complex. Ingenious. Verbal. Novelty seeking. Change oriented. Global. Independent. Adaptable.
ESTJ	**ESFJ**	**ENFJ**	**ENTJ**
Active organizer. Logical. Assertive. Fact minded. Decisive. Practical. Results oriented. Analytical. Systematic. Concrete. Critical. Responsible. Take charge. Common sense.	actively sociable. Warm. Harmonizer. Caring. Enthusiastic. Empathic. Practical. People-oriented. Responsible. Concrete. Orderly. Conscientious. Cooperative. Appreciative. Loyal.	Actively sociable. Enthusiastic. Harmonizer. Expressive. Warm. Idealistic. Empathic. Possibility-oriented. Insightful. Cooperative. Imaginative. Conscientious. Appreciative. Tactful.	Driving organizer. Planner. Vision focused. Decisive. Initiating. Conceptual. Strategic. Systematic. Assertive. Critical. Logical. Organized. Pursues improvement and achievement.

Self-Awareness

Research shows that self-awareness is more valuable than being smart—in the same manner, leaders who are self-aware have a greater chance achieving success in life. Self-reflection is an amazing tool that can help you deepen your inner knowledge and help you discover how to do your best work. It can also improve confidence and make you feel more capable, competent, and in control.

The following is a sample set of questions you can ask yourself every day to reflect and be more self-aware. Take 10-15 minutes a day to spend time on yourself, what you are thinking, where you are, and where you want to go. Incredible ideas arise when we take the time to analyze a little deeper about our own selves.

1. When am I at my best?
2. How do you spend the majority of your time?
3. What kind of person do I want to be today?
4. What situations make me feel terrible?
5. What activities am I doing when it feels like time is flying by?
6. What is working well in my life and work today?
7. If I had a magical wand, how would my life be better in three months?
8. If I change nothing, what will your life look like in three months?
9. What actions would make me proud of myself?
10. How do I deal with negative thoughts?

11. How do I stay grounded when I feel overwhelmed?
12. What motivates me to make progress?
13. What activities help me scape my reality?
14. Do you believe every thought you think?
15. Who, or what, always makes you laugh?

How to Create Affirmations

An affirmation is a powerful, positive statement that we repeat to ourselves that encourages us, motivate us, inspires us, and even gives us a little push when we need it most. Writing affirmations is fairly simple. It is just about knowing how to do it and knowing what to look for. I have designed a 15-question questionnaire to get you started. This is the same questionnaire I have used for years and it is very effective. The questionnaire is designed to provide mostly negative answers. You want to know the negative things happening in your life so that you can turn them around to positivity. The key to writing affirmations is to write the statement in the present tense using words like 'I am,' 'I do,' and 'I can.'

After finishing the questionnaire and getting all the negativity out of your system, start changing or replacing statements and turning them into positives by using words like 'because', or 'therefore'. For example, if a statement reads 'I am always so tired', change the statement into a positive and add an answer with the word 'because'. 'I always have energy because I get my rest at night'. 'I eat a lot of trash food' change it to 'I eat healthy food because I am strong, therefore, I have energy throughout the day'.

Remember, our thoughts reflect our internal beliefs. With time, practice, and repetition we can alter the information in the subconscious mind and before you know it, your affirmations will become your reality.

Pre-Affirmation Questionnaire

1. What is your current health condition? What is stopping you from being healthy? Any physical problems? What daily choice would you make different to have a healthier lifestyle?

2. Any sickness or conditions I need to be aware of? Write down the details?

3. How is your attitude on a scale 1-10? Your outlook on life? On others around you? Are you angry at yourself or life?

4. How positive or negative are you on a scale 1-10? Why?

5. Do you work? What do you do? How is your approach to your job, do you like it, why? Stressful, why?

6. What is your motivation in life? What drives you every morning to get out of bed and continue on?

7. What considerations are stopping you from reaching your potential? (considerations are THOUGHTS that stop you from reaching your goal. For example, you want to make more money, but it means you have to spend less time at home or work harder)

8. What limitations do you have? What things are stopping you from being the best person you can be? What things are stopping you from reaching your maximum potential as a person, mom, or dad?

9. What fears do you have? (fears are FEELINGS and EMOTIONS that may limit you. For example, if you are afraid of failing, making a fool out of yourself, disappointing someone)

10. What roadblocks do you have to be the person you want to be? (roadblocks are EXTERNAL circumstances that are out of your control. For example, you want a promotion and you are doing everything you can but it is out of your control)

11. How is the relationship with your husband or wife? With your parents? Siblings? Kids?

12. What is your confidence level to achieve what you want to achieve?

13. What are your short-term goals? Long term goals?

14. Talk to me about your sport? Mechanics? What's stopping you from being the best? Detail your areas of improvement?

15. Anything else that you feel you need to share that is stopping you from reaching complete happiness in life?

Sample of Powerful Words

The following are examples of words you can use to write powerful affirmations. There are many more powerful words, personalize your affirmations so they create a response for you.

Amazing	Enthusiastic	Leading
Awesome	Excited	Mindset
Achieve	Encourage	Motivated
Admire	Energetic	Now
Believe	Enjoy	Outstanding
Battle	Faithful	Patience
Confident	Fighter	Persistent
Concentrate	Finisher	Powerful
Control	Fabulous	Perseverance
Conquer	Goal	Reach
Determined	Grateful	Relentless
Dedicated	Happy	Strong
Drive	Imagination	Sensational
Desire	Inspiring	Spectacular
Empower	Joy	Successful

Sample Affirmations

"I am healthy and strong and every day I take care of my body because I am in total control of everything I do."

"I am always relaxed, positive, and confident because I trust myself and I believe I can achieve anything I set my mind to do."

"Every day I communicate effectively with myself and with the people around me because I am a positive leader."

"I am always in control of everything I do and everything I think about therefor I am the best version of myself every day."

"I work harder than anyone else because I always push myself beyond my limits and that makes me the best."

"I always give my absolute best on everything and I do and through my actions and decisions I make those around me proud."

"I am fearless, I am a warrior and I am always in control because I believe in myself."

"Anything is possible for he who believes." Mark 9:23

"I can do all things through Christ who gives me strength." Phil 4:13

Perceived Stress Scale

The Perceived Stress Scale is the most widely used psychological instrument for measuring the perception of stress. This assessment is not a diagnostic and it is only intended to measure the uncontrollable, unpredictable, and overload individuals find their life circumstances to be.

Take a few minutes to answer the following questions and then proceed to grade the assessment to find out about the level of stress you may currently have in your life.

0 = Never 1 = Almost Never 2 = Sometimes
3= Fairly Often 4= Very Often

1. In the last month, how often have you been upset because of something that happened unexpectedly?

    0   1   2   3   4

2. In the last month, how often have you felt that you Were unable to control the important things in your life?

    0   1   2   3   4

3. In the last month how often have you felt nervous and "stressed?"

    0   1   2   3   4

4. In the last month, how often have you felt confident about your ability to handle your personal problems?

    0   1   2   3   4

5. In the last month, how often have you felt that things were going your way?

0   1   2   3   4

6. In the last month, how often have you found that you could not cope with all the things that you had to do?

0   1   2   3   4

7. In the last month, how often have you been able to control irritations in your life?

0   1   2   3   4

8. In the last month, how often have you felt that you were on top of things?

0   1   2   3   4

9. In the last month, how often have you been angered because of things that were outside of your control?

0   1   2   3   4

10. In the last month, how often have you felt difficulties were piling up so high that you could not overcome them?

0   1   2   3   4

The Perceived Stress Scale has four positive answers, to obtain the results of this assessment, reverse the scores of items 4,5,7 and 8 so that if you scored 0 the number you will write down is 4 and same for the answers on questions 4,5,7 and 8 like this:

0=4, 1=3, 2=2, 3=1, 4=0

Results for answers: Results for answers:

1 = _____   4 = _____

2 = _____   5 = _____

3 = _____   7 = _____

6 = _____   8 = _____

9 = _____

10 = _____

Sum = _____   +   Sum = _____   Total = _____

If your result is 0 to 11, you have a low stress level, 12 to 24 your stress level is moderate, and 25 to 40 you have a high level of stress. Regardless of what your current stress level is, the beautiful thing about life is that we can always improve. The idea is to simply take a look at what your current stress level might be so that you can be aware of it and do whatever it is necessary to lower your stress.

Ho'oponopono

This process of forgiveness is meant to help you achieve pono- to be in perfect balance with all things in life and to live a life of righteousness. Ho'oponopono means 'correct a mistake' or 'make it right'. In a way, you are responsible for everything you see, touch, smell, taste, and hear and everything that happens to you, happens in your mind. You are responsible for anything and everything that you do, which also means, you can clear it, clean it, and through forgiveness, change it. The process of Ho'oponopono has four steps, repentance, forgiveness, gratitude, and love—or, "I am sorry," "forgive me," "thank you," and "I love you."

This technique is meant to be practiced daily and consistently in your own mind so you can be at peace with your decisions and the decisions of others.

Technique #1
Repentance, Forgiveness, Gratitude, and Love.

As mentioned before, you are responsible for anything and everything that is in your mind. Knowing this can lead to guilt, shame, anger, disappointment and many other negative feelings and emotions. To forgive yourself, or others, consistently practice this technique.

I am sorry for

_____

Forgive me for

_____

I am thankful for

_____

I love you because

_____

Technique #2
Stage Conversation

This technique requires you to have a 'mental' conversation or discussion with the person you hurt, or that hurt you, so that you can change the course of your life by forgiving and being forgiven.

1. Bring to mind any person with whom you do not feel fully aligned, supported by, someone you have hurt, or someone that has hurt you.
2. In your mind, build a platform or a stage in one of your happy places, and bring that person onto the platform or stage.
3. Imagine an infinite source of energy, love and healing power flowing from the whole sky down to your head. Allow that energy, love and healing power to flow inside of you, filling your own body first and then sending that energy to the person on stage. Fill that person's soul and body with energy, love and healing power.
4. Proceed to have a conversation or discussion with that person, this is the time to let the feelings, emotions and sensations you may have about this person, or yourself. Then, forgive the person and then make sure you hear them say they forgive

you as well (this process can take anywhere from 1 minute to hours depending on the situation).

5. Then, when you are done, let the person walk away from the stage. Allow the person to float away or disappear from the stage. As this person is beginning to fade away, cut the umbilical cord between you and the person so that you both do not depend on one another's pain any longer*.

6. Repeat steps 1-5 with anyone you feel incomplete or unaligned as many times as needed.

*The umbilical cord is a symbol of attachment as when a baby is attached in the mother's womb. The baby is dependent of the mother's umbilical cord for food and nutrients. The cutting of the umbilical cord separates the baby and the mother inside the womb and the baby can now live without being attached. The representation of cutting the umbilical cord between you and the person represents that you, or the person, no longer have to be dependent of one another's pain, shame, hate, guilt, anger or disappointment, and you are now both free to live your own life.

Relaxation Techniques

For all relaxation, meditation, and mindfulness techniques, read through the whole exercise before doing the exercise.

Deep Breath

Use this technique when starting to feel nervous or out of control. I encourage people to breath with the abdomen as sometimes a deep breath can send the wrong message to other people as it represents tension, stress, or feeling nervous. When practiced consistently, you can take deep breaths without anyone noticing.

1. Take a deep breath with your belly.
2. Hold it for several seconds.
3. As you exhale feel your body sinking down, letting go, and relaxing.
4. Repeat as necessary to achieve the desired level of relaxation.

Relax and Respond

I use this technique with a lot of athletes, but it is very effective to anyone who uses it. It is a two-breath tension control technique in which the first exhalation is the relaxation phase, and the second exhalation is the responding phase.

1. First breath: inhale through your nose.

2. Exhale slowly allowing your body to relax and feel as you start to sink down. Let go of all the tension.
3. Second breath: inhale through your nose.
4. Exhale slowly and respond with an affirmation about the activity. For example, concentrate on the hitter, I am a good writer, I can control the situation etc.

Exhalation Exercise

1. Sit or lay down comfortably, don't cross your legs or arms.
2. Passively observe your breathing and notice the coolness of the air as it enters your nose and feel the warmth of the air as you exhale.
3. As you exhale and during exhalation only, feel your body getting heavy. Choose a part of your body and feel as it starts to get heavy. Really focus on your shoulder, or your arm getting heavy. You have a 5-pound weight in that part of your body, and it gets heavy as you exhale. Continue to relax and let your body go. Really focus on that part of your body getting heavy. 4-6 breaths.
4. As you continue to exhale and only during the exhalation, feel your body slowing down. Feel sensations on your body and maybe you can feel the blood circulating through your veins, or you can hear your heartbeat. Continue focusing on this feeling and sensation as you exhale. Continue to relax and let your body go. 4-6 breaths.
5. As you exhale and during exhalation only, feel your body sinking down. Your head sinks down to the chair or floor. You feel the gravity pull you down towards the floor. Your feet are pushing against the carpet of the floor and the floor

is stopping you from continuing to sink down. Let go and continue to relax. 4-6 breaths.

6. As you exhale and during exhalation only, choose a part of your body and that part starts to get warm. Choose maybe an area of your body as your fingers or your toes and feel as during the exhalation your toes or fingers get warm. Continue to relax and let your body go. As you exhale the body part you chose continues to get warm. 4-6 breaths.

As you are ready to come out of the relaxation, breath 2-3 more times and keeping your eyes closed, flex, stretch and then open your eyes.

Autogenic Training

Developed by Johannes H. Schultz in 1932, Autogenic Training recreates the feelings of heaviness and warmth from hypnosis to reduce tension and stress. Autogenic training works through a series of self-statements about heaviness and warmth in different parts of the body. Through this process a positive effect is induced on the autonomic nervous system.

1. Focus your attention on your arms. Quietly and slowly as you breathe, repeat to yourself 6 times 'my arms are getting heavy' on the seventh time, quietly say to yourself 'I am completely calm'.

2. Refocus your attention on your arms. Quietly and slowly as you breathe repeat to yourself 6 times 'my arms are very warm' on the seventh time, quietly say to yourself 'I am completely calm'.

3. Focus your attention on your legs. Quietly and slowly as you breathe repeat to yourself 6 times 'my legs are getting heavy' on the seventh time, quietly say to yourself 'I am completely calm'.

4. Refocus your attention on your legs. Quietly and slowly as you breathe repeat to yourself 6 times 'my legs are very warm' on the seventh time, quietly say to yourself 'I am completely calm'.

5. As you continue breathing, quietly and slowly repeat to yourself 6 times 'my heartbeat is calm and regular' on the seventh time, quietly say to yourself 'I am completely calm'.

6. Continue breathing, quietly and slowly repeat to yourself 6 times 'my breathing is calm and regular' on the seventh time, quietly say to yourself 'I am completely calm'.

7. As you continue breathing and quietly and slowly repeat to yourself 6 times 'my abdomen is warm' on the seventh time, quietly say to yourself 'I am completely calm'.

8. Continue breathing, quietly and slowly repeat to yourself 6 times 'my forehead is pleasantly cool' on the seventh time, quietly say to yourself 'I am completely calm'.

9. Enjoy the feeling of relaxation, warmth, and heaviness and when you are ready to come out of relaxation, open your eyes.

Autogenic training may help you feel calm and relaxed in social and performance situations. Practicing autogenic training often and consistently will train your mind to relax.

Visualization

Visualization techniques have been used by successful people to visualize their desired outcomes for many years. The daily practice of visualizing your goals as already complete can rapidly accelerate your achievement of those goals or ambitions.

Visualizing your goals and desires has four powerful benefits:

1. It activates your creative subconscious.
2. It programs your brain.
3. It activates the law of attraction and,
4. It builds your internal motivation.

Visualization is actually quite simple. As you are in a comfortable position, close your eyes and imagine as vividly as you can, what you would be looking at if the goal you have were already completed. Imagine being inside of yourself, looking out through your eyes at the ideal result.

Mental Rehearsal

Most athletes use a technique called mental rehearsal, which was originally introduced to the world by the Russians in the 1960s. If you make this part of your daily routine, you will be amazed at how much improvement you will see in your life.

1. Imagine sitting in a movie theater, the lights dim, and then the movie starts. It is a movie of you doing perfectly whatever it is that you want to do better. See as much detail as you can create, including your clothing, the expression on your face, small body movements, the environment, and any other people that might be around. Add in any sounds you would be hearing — traffic, music, other people talking, cheering. And finally, recreate in your body any feelings you think you would be experiencing as you engage in this activity.

2. Get out of your chair, walk up to the screen, open a door in the screen and enter into the movie. Now experience the whole thing again from inside of yourself, looking out through your eyes. This is called an "embodied image" rather than a "distant image." It will deepen the impact of the experience. Again, see everything in vivid detail, hear the sounds you would hear, and feel the feelings you would feel.

3. Finally, walk back out of the screen that is still showing the picture of you performing perfectly, return to your seat in the theater, reach out and grab the screen and shrink it down to the size of a cracker. Then, bring this miniature screen up to your mouth, chew it up and swallow it. Imagine that each tiny piece — just like a hologram — contains the full picture of you performing well. Imagine all these little screens traveling down into your stomach and out through the bloodstream into every cell of your body. Then imagine that every cell of your body is lit up with a movie of you performing perfectly. It's like one of those appliance stores where 50 televisions are all tuned to the same channel.

Meditation

Guided Imagery

Imagery and visualization are very similar as both use the imagination for a specific purpose, however, visualization focuses more on a definite outcome. Guided imagery is more relevant for managing stress.

1. Find a quiet place to sit down or lay down.
2. Close your eyes and breathe slowly and deeply.
3. Once you are feeling relaxed, picture yourself in the most peaceful environment you can imagine. It can be an imagined place or a memory that is meaningful to you.
4. When you are at the place you are imagining, use all of your senses. Imagery's effectiveness relies on using the senses. For example, imagining yourself in a relaxing tropical beach:
   a. Feel the sun in your body
   b. Touch the towel you are laying on
   c. Smell the ocean water
   d. See the birds flying by
   e. Taste the lemonade you are drinking
5. Stay in your relaxed scene for as long as you feel comfortable, as long as your schedule allows, or simply as long as you want.

6. When you are ready to come out of the imagery, sit quietly and let your mind turn back to the present moment or situation at hand.

Body Scan Meditation

In body scan relaxation, you tense a group of muscles as you breathe in, and you relax the same group of muscles as you breathe out. You work on your muscle groups in a certain order.

1. Breathe in, and tense the first muscle group, hard but not to the point of pain or cramping for 5 to 10 seconds.
2. Breathe out, and suddenly completely relax the muscle group, make sure you do not relax it gradually.
3. Relax for 10-20 seconds before you work on the next muscle group. Notice the difference between how your muscles feel when they are tense and how they feel when they are relaxed.
4. When you are finished with all the muscle groups, count backward from 5 to 1 and bring your focus back to the present.

Muscle groups:

1. Hands: clench them
2. Wrists and forearms: extend them and bend your hands back at the wrist
3. Biceps and upper arms: clench your hands into fists, bend your arm at the elbows and flex your biceps
4. Shoulders: shrug them or raise them towards your ears
5. Forehead: wrinkle it into a deep frown
6. Around the eyes: close your eyes as hard as you can
7. Cheeks and jaw: press your lips together tightly

8. Back of the neck: press the back of your neck against floor or chair
9. Front of the neck: touch your chin to your chest
10. Chest: take a deep breath and hold it for 5-10 seconds
11. Back: arch your back up and away from floor or chair
12. Stomach: suck it into a tight knot
13. Hips and buttocks: press your buttocks together tightly
14. Thighs: clench them hard
15. Lower legs: point your toes toward your face then point your toes away

After you have learned how to tense and relax each muscle group and you realize you have tension in a specific part of the body, you can practice tensing and relaxing that muscle without having to go through the whole routine.

Transcendental Meditation

The journey of Transcendental Meditation begins by finding a certified TM teacher and taking courses to learn the practice. Teachers are certified by Maharishi Foundation USA, a federally recognized non-profit organization.

Here's what a typical practice of Transcendental Meditation looks like:

1. Sit in a comfortable chair with your feet on the ground and hands in your lap. Leave your legs and arms uncrossed.
2. Close your eyes and take a few deep breaths to relax the body.
3. Open your eyes, and then close them again. Your eyes will remain closed during the 20-minute practice.

4. Repeat a mantra in your mind. This is typically a Sanskrit sound learned from a TM teacher.

5. When you recognize you're having a thought, simply return to the mantra.

6. After 20 minutes, begin to move your fingers and toes to ease yourself back to the world.

7. Open your eyes.

8. Sit for a few more minutes until you feel ready to continue with your day.

Mindfulness

5 Senses Awareness Mindfulness

This mindfulness technique requires you to tune into your five senses (sight, hearing, touch, smell, and taste) after the completion of whatever task you are doing. At the completion of the task, name two or three examples of the things you notice for each sense. For example, when you drink any beverage, you may notice:

- The flavor of the beverage in your tongue.
- The smell coming through your nostrils.
- The refreshing feeling.
- The sounds as you drink.
- The way you hold the beverage.
- The feeling of holding the beverage.

This technique can help you increase your present-moment awareness and you can practice in everyday activities; even those you have done thousands of times. Each time, you might notice new things about where you are, what you do, and the space you are in. You are being mindful.

Mindful Eating

This technique is about mindfully eating any kind of food you desire.

- Slow down and sense it.
- Smile between bites.
- Use all your senses to see it, touch it, smell it. Sense it.
- Savor each bite, the texture, the taste, how it feels in your mouth.
- Swallow the food and smile.
- Do and repeat the process for each bite you take.

10-Week Mentally Strong Program

As promised, the following is an introductory 10-week mental training program for you to get started in becoming mentally stronger. You are to start this program any day of the week, but make sure you work on the one topic for the week, the entire week. Each week, you will add a new concept to work on and you will continue to work on the concepts for the previous weeks.

Week One

1. *Be aware and replace your thoughts.*

Replace all negativity with positivity. Identify negative thoughts and negative thinking patterns and replace them with positive thinking patterns. Turn all negativity in your head, to positivity.

Week Two

1. *Start working on your relaxations.*
2. Be aware and replace your thoughts.

Sign up at www.thechoicetobelieve.com and get the free 5-minute relaxation audio. Relax for five minutes, three times per day; in the afternoon, late afternoon, and before going to bed. Set alarms in your phone at the exact times you are going to be relaxing every day.

During relaxation, stay in control to stay awake. If you happen to miss a relaxation, just do the next one. Do not do relaxations in a row. Give yourself a minimum of a few hours in between each relaxation and without exceeding three guided relaxations in one day.

Week Three

1. *Create your affirmations.*
2. Relax 3 times a day for five minutes.
3. Be aware and Replace your thoughts.

Follow the steps in the appendix and create affirmations for yourself. Read your affirmations a minimum of 8 times per day. Remember that affirmations are meant to stimulate positive feelings, emotions, and sensations in you. Read your affirmations following this schedule.

- 2 times when you first wake up.
- 2 times after your early afternoon relaxation.
- 2 times after your late afternoon relaxation.
- 2 times after your 'before going to sleep' relaxation.

You can read affirmations as many times as you want throughout the day in addition to the schedule mentioned above.

Week Four

1. *Remove the words 'no', 'don't', and 'can't' from your vocabulary.*
2. Relax 3 times a day for five minutes.
3. Read affirmations throughout the day.
4. Be aware and replace your thoughts.

You are to go deeper into thought replacement and be aware of the words, 'no,' 'don't,' and 'can't' and replace them with 'I am,' 'I do,' and 'I can.'

Do the Chevreul Pendulum Exercise and see for yourself the amazing power of the brain. At the order of your mind, your body will begin to react. Most people see the pendulum move in the direction they want, within seconds. However, the exercise can take up to a few minutes for other people, but it will react.

Now, do the exercise again, but this time, instead of giving a positive order to the pendulum, give the pendulum a negative order such as 'don't' move sideways. What happens? The pendulum will move the exact same way that you asked not to move. Why? Because as we gather information, the brain is going to generalize, distort, and delete information. This is not always a bad thing, but when it comes to negativity, the body will react to a negative affirmation as well. Therefore, negative words will influence your brain and your body in a negative way.

Generalization

The following paragraph is an example of generalization. When you look only at the first and last letter of the word, your brain generalizes all the letters in the middle and allow you to understand what it says.

I cdnuolt bilevee that I cluod aulaclty uesdnatnrd what I was rdanieg. The phaonmneal pweor of the hmuan mnid, aoccdrnig to a rscheearch at Cmabrigde Uinervtisy, it dseno't mtaetr in what oerdr the ltteres in a word are, the olny iproamtnt tihng is that the frsit and last ltteer be in the rghit pclae. The rset can be a taotl mses and you can still raed it whotuit a pboerlm. This is bcuseae the huamn mnid deos not raed ervey lteter by istlef, but the word as a wlohe. Azanmig huh?

Real life examples of generalization occur, for example, when someone is speaking, and your brain starts to connect the dots as to what the person is going to say next. If the person is saying A, B, C, D... your brain connects the fact that the next thing the person is going to say is E. However, in a real conversation, that may not necessarily be true. We assume and think the person is going to say something, but often we have absolutely no idea what they will say. Your brain generalizes the information and when you generalize, you may miss on important information.

Distortion

Similar to generalizations, once your brain realizes a pattern, it will understand the pattern and allow you to see something you may have missed before. Take a look at the following example:

7H15 M3554G3 53RV35 7O PR0V3 H0W 0UR M1ND5 C4N D0 4M4Z1NG 7H1NG5! 1MPR3551V3 7H1NG5! 1N 7H3 B3G1NN1NG 17 WA5 H4RD BU7 N0W, 0N 7H15 LIN3 Y0UR M1ND 1S R34D1NG 17 4U70M471C4LLY W17H 0U7 3V3N 7H1NK1NG 4B0U7 17, B3 PROUD! 0NLY C3R741N P30PL3 C4N R3AD 7H15.

If you have no idea what the message says, replace the numbers with letters, for example the '7' is a 'T', the '1' is an 'I', and the '5' is an 'S'. So, the first word reads THIS. As you continue to read knowing and understanding the pattern, your mind will automatically read it.

Real life examples of distortions occur when for example, someone sees a shadow, or the clouds and associate the shape of such with other objects or images. A shadow might look like the shape of a face, or someone might see the figure of a house in the clouds. You may not be able to see what other people see, and vice versa and because of distortions, we miss on certain information.

Deletion

Read the following sentence out loud.

NEW YORK IN
IN THE WINTER

Did you realize that the sentence actually has the word 'IN' two times? If you didn't, don't worry, about 65% of people in the world don't see it. Why? The brain doesn't need it to complete the sentence, so it deletes it. In the same manner, when we use words like 'no,' 'don't,' and 'can't,' the brain will delete certain words and we may actually be giving ourselves a negative order without realizing it. For example:

I don't want to drink

If the brain happens to delete the word 'don't,' it will read:

I want to drink

If the brain happens to delete any other word, the word 'don't' will remain in the sentence and because it is a negative word, it will affect the body in a negative way—through the pendulum example.

Real life examples of deletions occur frequently, for example when you tell yourself not to forget something from the supermarket. Many times, you get everything else you needed, except the one thing you 'didn't' want to forget. For example:

Don't forget the milk

You go to the supermarket and forget the milk; or anything else you tell yourself to not forget. Many times you end up forgetting the very same thing you didn't want to forget. Sound familiar?

Week Five

1. *Stop blaming, complaining, and making excuses.*
2. Remove the words 'no', 'don't', and 'can't' from your vocabulary.
3. Relax 3 times a day for five minutes.
4. Read affirmations throughout the day.
5. Be aware and replace your thoughts.

You need to be aware to identify when your mind wants to blame, complain, and make excuses about any situation, or event. Be responsible for yourself, what you think and what you do. If for example, you are not doing the three relaxations per day, or following the direction of this mental program, be responsible and get back on track.

Week Six

1. *Eliminate the stress from your life.*
2. Stop blaming, complaining, and making excuses.
3. Remove the words 'no,' 'don't,' and 'can't' from your vocabulary.
4. Relax 3 times a day for five minutes.
5. Read affirmations throughout the day.
6. Be aware and replace your thoughts.

You are to identify what leads you to feel overwhelmed or stressed. Once you identify the stressors in your life, deal with them so that they are no longer influencing your mind. If, for example, it stresses you to have a dirty room, the stressor is all the mess in the room. Clean your room and make sure that moving forward you put things away where they belong in the first place so that your room remains clean all the time, therefore eliminating the stress that comes from a dirty room.

Week Seven

1. *Replace the words 'have to' and 'need to' with 'want to' and 'get to.'*
2. Eliminate the stress from your life
3. Stop blaming, complaining, and making excuses.
4. Remove the words 'no', 'don't', and 'can't' from your vocabulary
5. Relax 3 times a day for five minutes
6. Read affirmations throughout the day
7. Be aware and replace your thoughts

You are to pay attention to how you think and how you speak and every time you catch yourself thinking or saying the words 'have to' or 'need to' you are to replace them with either 'want to' or 'get to'. The bottom line is, if your mind tells you there is something you have to do, in reality, you don't have to do it, but there will be consequences if you don't do it. So, you are better off using powerful words that will encourage you or make you feel different. For example, say out loud the following sentences:

- I have to go to work tomorrow.
- I need to go to a dinner tonight.

Then, say out loud the following sentences:

- I want to go to work tomorrow.
- I get to go to a dinner tonight.

Do you feel the difference in your body language, pitch, voice, and tone? If you pay attention, you can actually feel the difference in your heart and your body. When you use positive and powerful words, in this case 'want to' and 'get to' the words create a sense of peace in your heart and body.

Week Eight

1. *Pay attention to your attitude.*
2. Replace the words 'have to' and 'need to' with 'want to' and 'get to.'
3. Eliminate the stress from your life.
4. Stop blaming, complaining, and making excuses.
5. Remove the words 'no', 'don't', and 'can't' from your vocabulary.
6. Relax 3 times a day for five minutes.
7. Read affirmations throughout the day.
8. Be aware and replace your thoughts.

You are to pay attention to your attitude by being aware of your thinking patterns and making the decision to turn your mentality into one or all of the following:

- Kobe- whatever it takes
- SEALs- failure is not an option
- Nike- "Just Do It."

Remember that your attitude reflects your leadership and your attitude towards any situation or circumstance will either make you or break you. You want to have the best chance to succeed, you have to turn your attitude around as soon as possible. It is okay to have negative feelings and emotions; a great attitude is to accept those feelings and emotions and go back to be your normal self as quickly as possible.

Week Nine

1. *Have fun and enjoy everything you do.*
2. Pay attention to your attitude.
3. Replace the words 'have to' and 'need to' with 'want to' and 'get to.'
4. Eliminate the stress from your life.
5. Stop blaming, complaining, and making excuses.
6. Remove the words 'no', 'don't', and 'can't' from your vocabulary.
7. Relax 3 times a day for five minutes.
8. Read affirmations throughout the day.
9. Be aware and replace your thoughts.

You are to find a way to enjoy everything that life has to offer—the good, the bad, and the ugly. Having fun and enjoying what you do is a decision you make in your mind.

Week Ten

1. *Turn yourself into a problem-solving machine.*
2. Have fun and enjoy everything you do.
3. Pay attention to your attitude.
4. Replace the words 'have to' and 'need to' with 'want to' and 'get to.'
5. Eliminate the stress from your life.
6. Stop blaming, complaining, and making excuses.

7. Remove the words 'no', 'don't', and 'can't' from your vocabulary.
8. Relax 3 times a day for five minutes.
9. Read affirmations throughout the day.
10. Be aware and replace your thoughts.

The final week of the 10-week program and every day moving forward you are to think in terms of 'what am I going to do about it?' Your mind will have a tendency to:

- Gear towards negativity,
- To see problems,
- Tension,
- Stress,
- Roadblocks,
- Fears, and
- Limitations.

Instead of asking yourself the questions 'why?' ask yourself 'what you are going to do about it' and turn any of the mentioned above mental blockages into solutions. And every day, enjoy what it feels like to be on your way to becoming the best version of yourself with a stronger mentality.

For information in continuing your journey and personally work with me, contact me at www.thechoicetobelieve.com.

Bibliography

"Cognitive Flexibility." *Cognitive Flexibility - an Overview | ScienceDirect Topics*, www.sciencedirect.com/topics/neuroscience/cognitive-flexibility.

Eurich, Tasha. "What Self-Awareness Really Is (and How to Cultivate It)." *Harvard Business Review*, 23 Apr. 2018, hbr.org/2018/01/ what-self-awareness-really-is-and-how-to-cultivate-it.

James Clear. *Habits Guide: How to Build Good Habits and Break Bad Ones.* 3 Feb. 2020, jamesclear.com/habits.

Porter, Nicole. *Did You Know...95% of Disease Is Stress-Related?* 17 Nov. 2019, www.nicoleporterwellness.com/know-95-disease-stress-related/.

Robins, Ellie. "The Secret Benefit of Routines. It Won't Surprise You." *The Orange Dot*, The Orange Dot, 19 July 2017, www.headspace.com/ blog/2016/08/22/the-secret-benefit-of-routines-it-wont-surprise-you/.

Shortsleeve, Cassie. "How to Break Bad Habits, According to Science." *Time*, Time, 28 Aug. 2018, time.com/5373528/break-bad-habit-science/.

Turner, Ash, et al. "1 Billion More Phones Than People In The World! BankMyCell." *BankMyCell*, 7 Aug. 2020, www.bankmycell.com/blog/ how-many-phones-are-in-the-world.

Westmeria. *Understanding the Freeze Stress Response.* westmeriacounselling. co.uk/understanding-the-freeze-stress-response/.